mentor Lernhilfe

Englisch

5. Klasse

Grammatik und Wortschatz, Teil 2: Für das zweite Halbjahr

Rainer Iwen

Mit Übungen und Lösungen

In Zusammenarbeit mit Langenscheidt

mentor
Eine Klasse besser.

Über den Autor:
Rainer Iwen, Realschulrektor und Studienleiter für Englisch am Institut für Praxis und Theorie der Schule (Landesinstitut für Lehrerfortbildung)

Projektleitung:
Dorothea Leiser

Redaktion:
Eva-Maria Gärtner, Geraldine Tahmassebi

Illustrationen:
Jutta Bauer, Christiane Hansen, Vivien Thiessen, alle Hamburg

Layout:
Sabine Nasko, München

Umwelthinweis: Gedruckt auf chlorfrei gebleichtem Papier.

Printed in Austria
www.mentor.de

ISBN-13: 978-3-580-65539-6
ISBN-10: 3-580-65539-6

1. 2. 3. 4. 5. / 10 09 08 07 06

Inhalt

Willkommen!

Hallo, liebe Schülerin, lieber Schüler,

du willst etwas für bessere Noten in Englisch tun?
Gratuliere – den ersten Schritt hast du damit schon geschafft!

Bei den weiteren Schritten wird dich diese mentor Lernhilfe unterstützen: Du findest hier alle wichtigen **Grammatikregeln** und **Vokabeln,** dazu viele abwechslungsreiche **Übungen**, die wirklich Spaß machen. Und du lernst den lustigen **Fred** kennen, der dir dabei helfen wird.

Du kannst das Buch als Wiederholungskurs von vorne bis hinten durcharbeiten, du kannst aber auch einzelne Kapitel auswählen, die du in der Schule gerade brauchst. Ganz wie du willst! Du kannst mit diesem Buch nämlich ganz alleine arbeiten, ohne Stress.

Besorge dir gleich
- ein paar bunte Stifte zum Anstreichen und Ausmalen,
- ein Extraheft für längere Übungen,
- Bleistift und Radiergummi zum Verbessern.

Die **Lösungen** zu den Übungen findest du hinten im Buch. Aber nicht spicken! Versuche es erst selbst, bevor du nachschaust. Am meisten lernst du, wenn deine Fehler sorgfältig verbesserst und überlegst, warum du sie gemacht hast.

Und zum Abschluss führt dich eine spannende **Textbook Rally** nochmals kreuz und quer durch das ganze Buch – du wirst staunen, was du alles gelernt hast!

Wir wünschen dir ganz viel Erfolg in der 5. Klasse!

Rainer Iwen und der mentor Verlag

PS: Wenn dir dieses Buch gefallen hat, würden wir uns riesig freuen, dich in den nächsten Bänden wiederzusehen! Noch mehr Übungen für die 5. Klasse findest du übrigens in dem Band fürs erste Halbjahr.

So funktioniert's!

Grammar In diesen blauen Kästen stehen wichtige Erklärungen zur **Grammatik,** die du meist schon aus der Schule kennst. Lerne bzw. wiederhole sie sorgfältig, denn die brauchst du wirklich!

Words Hier sind **Vokabeln** übersichtlich zusammengestellt: Auch die solltest du beherrschen!

Info Hier gibt es weitere **Informationen** zu verschiedenen Themen.

Reading Hier findest du spannende, lustige, interessante Geschichten, Gedichte oder andere Texte zum **Lesen**. Du wirst staunen, was du schon alles auf Englisch verstehst! Und es macht gar nichts aus, wenn du noch nicht alle Wörter kennst.

Dialogue Hier geht's ums **Sprechen**: Präge dir diese Ausdrücke und Redewendungen gut ein und trau dich, sie bei der nächsten Gelegenheit in der Schule oder außerhalb anzuwenden!

! Hier heißt es **„Aufgepasst!“**, denn wir geben dir einen Tipp oder weisen dich auf einen Stolperstein hin.

Und ich bin **Fred**, ich helfe dir – versprochen!

1. Words

1.1 Words for pictures

Write the correct word for each picture.

Schau dir die Bilder an und trage die englischen Wörter ein, die du kennst.

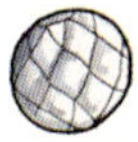 volleyball ....

 ra ....

 ....

 ....

 b ....

 ....

 ....

 ....

sh ....

 sh ....

 ....

 ....

 ....

 ....

 ....

 ....

 ....

 over ....

 ....

 ....

 ....

 ....

 ....

 ....

 ....

....

 ....

 ....

 ....

 Fr ....

1.2 Wordfields

Write the words in your exercise book.

boss star babysitter jet golf
cassette fair bubble gum video
jazz shop camping killer computer
music box gentleman pop boy
song jeep TV cornflakes fit
body building manager inline skates
walkman drink milk shake supermarket
down trip highway party
hot dog playboy out hobby
city T-shirt service clever
team show cotton gangster
teenager volleyball toast
mountain bike jeans steak quiz
rock'n'roll popcorn stewardess
oldie motel job clown overall
girl foul lady sandwich story
shorts baby hit

Welche englischen Wörter gehören wohin? Schreibe unter die passenden Stichwörter in dein Heft.

Sport	Musik	Essen/ Trinken	Freizeit/ Vergnügen	Eigen-schaften
golf		milk shake		fair

Kleidung	Geschäfts-leben/Berufe	Fernsehen/ Film	Verkehr/ Straße/Stadt	Menschen
			mountain bike	

1.3 The word game

Play this game with a friend.

– Throw a dice and count the squares.
– Make a sentence with the word in that square.
– The winner is the first person with the most correct sentences.

Start	1 like	2 two	3 three	4 London	5 can
6 colour	7 your	8 fifteen	9 eighteen	10 and	11 blue
12 green	13 yellow	14 park	15 cat	16 coke	17 banana
18 table tennis	19 is	20 her	21 Thursday	22 seven	23 milk
24 old	25 car	26 queen	27 bed	28 budgie	29 on
30 crocodile	31 water	32 ice	33 aunt	34 hamburger	35 Goodbye

Words

2. Months of the Year

2.1

Do you know the names of the months?

Fill in.

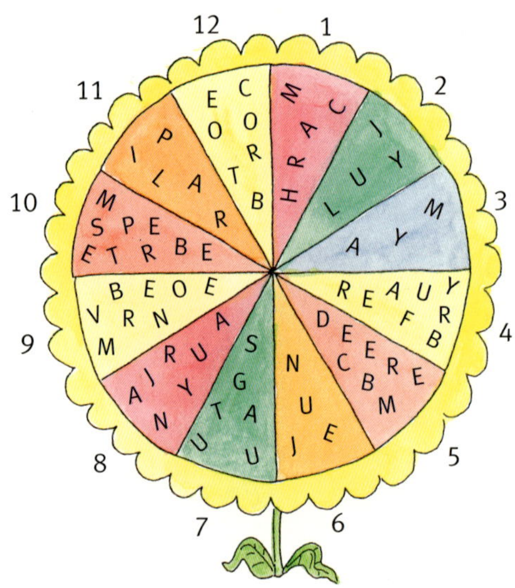

1. March	2.	3. ....
4.	5.	6. ....
7.	8.	9. ....
10.	11.	12. ....

2.2 The months

Fill in the names of the months.

January ……… ……… ………

……… ……… ……… ………

……… ……… ……… ………

2.3 Which month is it?

Fill in!

January is the first ……… month of the year.

……… is the second month of the year.

……… is the fourth month of the year.

August is the ……… month of the year.

September is the ……… month of the year.

……… is the twelfth month of the year.

……… is the fifth month of the year.

……… is the eleventh month of the year.

March is the ……… month of the year.

Info

The date

You can **write** the date like this:

You can **say** the date like this:

Dialogue

Talking about the date

Welches Datum haben wir heute?	→	What's the date today?
Wir haben den ersten Mai.	→	It's May (the) first. or It's the first of May.

2.4 What date is it?

Match the numbers and months in the two boxes with colours. Then write the dates.

third twentieth eighth ninth second thirtieth first thirty-first fourteenth twenty-second fifth

February May September June January October April July November August December March

2. 10. [green]	the second of October	October 2nd
20. 2. [blue]		
1. 1. [white]		
30. 3. [yellow]		
3. 11. [red]		
31. 12. [pink]		
14. 5. [brown]		

Now write the dates that are left.

22. 9.		
9. 7.		
5. 4.		
8. 8.		
2. 6.		

2.5 A calendar

Look at the calendar and complete the sentences.

	JANUARY	FEBRUARY	MARCH	APRIL	MAY	JUNE
S	31 3 10 17 24	7 14 21 28	7 14 21 28	4 11 18 25	30 2 9 16 23	6 13 20 27
M	4 11 18 25	1 8 15 22	1 8 15 22 29	5 12 19 26	31 3 10 17 24	7 14 21 28
T	5 12 19 26	2 9 16 23	2 9 16 23 30	6 13 20 27	4 11 18 25	1 8 15 22 29
W	6 13 20 27	3 10 17 24	3 10 17 24 31	7 14 21 28	5 12 19 26	2 9 16 23 30
Th	7 14 21 28	4 11 18 25	4 11 18 25	1 8 15 22 29	6 13 20 27	3 10 17 24
F	1 8 15 22 29	5 12 19 26	5 12 19 26	2 9 16 23 30	7 14 21 28	4 11 18 25
S	2 9 16 23 30	6 13 20 27	6 13 20 27	3 10 17 24	1 8 15 22 29	5 12 19 26

	JULY	AUGUST	SEPTEMBER	OCTOBER	NOVEMBER	DECEMBER
S	4 11 18 25	1 8 15 22 29	5 12 19 26	31 3 10 17 24	7 14 21 28	5 12 19 26
M	5 12 19 26	2 9 16 23 30	6 13 20 27	4 11 18 25	1 8 15 22 29	6 13 20 27
Tu	6 13 20 27	3 10 17 24 31	7 14 21 28	5 12 19 26	2 9 16 23 30	7 14 21 28
W	7 14 21 28	4 11 18 25	1 8 15 22 29	6 13 20 27	3 10 17 24	1 8 15 22 29
Th	1 8 15 22 29	5 12 19 26	2 9 16 23 30	7 14 21 28	4 11 18 25	2 9 16 23 30
F	2 9 16 23 30	6 13 20 27	3 10 17 24	1 8 15 22 29	5 12 19 26	3 10 17 24 31
S	3 10 17 24 31	7 14 21 28	4 11 18 25	2 9 16 23 30	6 13 20 27	4 11 18 25

● Fred ◆ Mum ■ Aunt Mary ◊ Pam ○ Dad

Mum's birthday is on the twenty-second of September.

Dad's birthday is on ....

Fred's birthday is on ....

Aunt Mary's birthday is on ....

Pam's birthday is on ....

> Bei der Frage, wann man geboren wurde, gebraucht man im Englischen immer ***was/were*** (Past Tense).

!

2.6 Over to you: Talking about your family

Answer the questions.

When is your birthday? On the .... of ....

When is your mother's birthday? On the .... of ....

When is your father's birthday? On the .... of ....

When were you born? In .... (year).

When was your father born? In ....

When was your mother born? In ....

2.7 Birthday rhyme time

Fill in.

dish – Platte / Teller

The candles are lit.
The cake's on its dish.
It's time to make my
birthday ....!

Today's the date!
I'm feeling great!
What day's today?
It's my ....!

It's fun to mix
It's fun to make,
It's fun to bake
A birthday ....!

2.8 Pen friends

Michael and Claudia are pen friends. Michael lives in Edinburgh, Scotland. Claudia lives in Kiel, Germany. Fill in the blanks.

Dear ...., 

Many thanks for your ....  . I hope you and your family are well. We are all fine. I'm writing this letter on .... 

of January.

It's ....  here now. It's ....  a lot at the moment. I can't ....  this .... 

, so I'm staying at home listening to  ...., watching ....  and writing this letter. Next .... 

is my ....  and Mum is making me a big ....  .
She's got eleven ....  for it. All my friends will come to my .... 

and we'll ....  and ....  . My birthday also means more ....  .

Please write soon!

Best wishes

Michael

2.9 A birthday invitation

Read the invitation card aloud.

invitation – Einladung

Invitation

Dear Susan,

It's my birthday next Saturday and I'm going to have a party. Can you come? I hope so! We'll have fun. There will be food, lots of games and lots of prizes. The party is at 19 Portland Road. It starts at four 'o clock p.m. See you on Saturday.

Lots of love
Barbara

2.10 Over to you: My birthday party

Write an invitation card for a birthday party.

The party is at 25 Regent Street. It's on Saturday, 1st April at 4.30 p.m.

Reading

2.11 Susan's birthday

Read the text and answer the questions.

October the 11th is a great day for Susan. It's her birthday. She's eleven. In the morning she opens her birthday cards. She has seventeen cards from her family and her friends. From her mum and dad she gets a new bike, and from her brother Bob a wonderful book about horses. Susan likes horses very much. Aunt Mary gives her £ 25. "You can buy some jeans or T-shirts with it," she says. Susan is very happy. At half past three there's a big birthday party at her house. All her friends are there. They eat birthday cake and play a lot of games. They also dance to Susan's favourite music. Susan dances with Peter. At nine o'clock she is very tired – and very happy. "What a great day," she thinks.

1. When is Susan's birthday? ....
2. How old is she? ....
3. What does she do in the morning? ....
4. How many cards does she get? ....
5. What does she get from her family? ....
6. What do the boys and girls do at Susan's party? ....

2.12 Over to you: What do you do on your birthday?

Write sentences in your exercise book about your birthday.

My birthday:

- go to the cinema
- be at home
- invite friends
- play games
- go out and have a picnic
- dance
- have a party
- visit my grandmother
- eat cake
- listen to music

3. The Auxiliary *can* / Das Hilfsverb „können“

3.1 Spare time activities

Match the activities below to the pictures. Write under the pictures.

1 ....

2 ....

3 ....

4 ....

5 ....

6 ....

7 ....

8 ....

9 ....

10 ....

11 ....

12 ....

play football – ride a bike – fish – skate – ski – swim – sail – dance –
play tennis – organise his stamps – climb trees – ride a horse

Now write down in your exercise book what Fred can do.

Example:
Fred can play football.

Grammar

Das Hilfsverb *can* drückt eine Fähigkeit oder Unfähigkeit aus. Es hat nur eine Form für alle Personen und kann nicht alleine stehen. Man muss immer ein Verb im Infinitiv (Grundform)hinzufügen, außer bei den Kurzantworten. Die verneinte Form heißt *cannot* oder kurz *can’t*.

Positive Statement		
I You He/She/It We You They	can	swim

Negation		
I You He/She/It We You They	cannot can’t	swim

3.2 Fred’s broken arm

Fred has broken his arm. Which things do you think he can and which things can’t he do?

play the guitar – climb trees – wash his ears – go to school – open bottles – go to bed – do his homework – take a shower – use his computer – eat with a spoon – go out for a walk –

spoon – Löffel

Example:

Fred can’t climb trees with his broken arm.
Fred can go out for a walk.

....

....

....

....

....

Go on in your exercise book.

3.3 Animals

Describe what the animals can do or can't do. Write in your exercise book.

fly – swim – run fast – jump – hear well – pull carts – climb trees – sing – see well – smell very well – catch mice – eat other animals – live without water – eat bananas – bark

Example: Rabbits can run very fast but they can't see very well.

3.4 I'm thinking of an animal

Bob is thinking of an animal (a dog) and Ann has to guess it. Fill in the gaps and finish the dialogue.

Du kennst doch das Spiel? Einer denkt sich ein Tier und der andere versucht es durch Fragen zu erraten. (Bob denkt an einen Hund)

Bob: I'm thinking of an animal.
Ann: Can it climb trees, Bob?
Bob: No, it can't.

Ann: .... it fly?

Bob: No, ...

Ann: .... it walk on two legs?

Bob: No, ...

Ann: .... it hear well?

Bob: Yes, ...

Go on in your exercise book.

Dialogue 3.5

Classroom talk

What do you or your teacher say in class when ...? Look at the phrases below.

du etwas nicht verstehst — I can't understand that.

du Hilfe brauchst

du etwas nicht gut sehen kannst

dein Lehrer etwas wiederholen soll

du etwas nicht tun kannst, weil es zu schwierig ist

du wissen willst, wie etwas geschrieben wird

du das Fenster öffnen möchtest

dein Lehrer deine Hausaufgaben sehen will

du an die Tafel schreiben willst

du etwas ausgesprochen haben willst

I can't do this. It's too difficult. – Can you say that again, please? – Can you help me, please? – I can't see it very well. – I can't understand that. – Can you show me your homework, please? – Can I open the window, please? – Can you pronounce that word, please? – Can I write that word on the board, please? – Can you spell that word, please?

Besonderheiten der Schreibung

Grammar

1. Im Normalfall wird an die Grundform des Verbs ein **-s** angehängt:
   to ask – he asks
   to write – she writes
   to happen – it happens
2. Endet das Verb auf einen **Zischlaut**, so wird **-es** angehängt:
   to watch – he watches
   to fetch – he fetches
   to miss – it misses
3. Endet das Verb auf **Konsonant und -y**, dann wird -y zu **-ie** und ein **-s** angehängt:
   to fly – it flies
   to hurry – she hurries
4. Endet das Verb auf **Vokal und -y**, dann bleibt das -y und es wird einfach ein **-s** angehängt:
   to play – she plays
   to say – he says

Ausnahme: *I go – he goes* *I do – he does*

5.2 The 3rd person singular verb machine

Fill in the correct forms.

1. you say ... he / she says
2. they fly ...
3. we get ...
4. I fetch ...
5. you do ...
6. I buy ...
7. they catch ...
8. we cook ...
9. you hurry ...
10. I go ...
11. you kiss ...

Fred writes.

5·3 European children

Write sentences about the children.

	Katrin	Mustafa	Sven	Paula
to live	Munich	Hamburg	Oslo	Madrid
to come from	Germany	Turkey	Norway	Spain
to speak	German English	Turkish German	Norwegian German	Spanish English
to play	table tennis	football	volleyball	tennis
to collect	stickers	CDs	comics	posters
to like	sweets	dancing	swimming	riding
to hate	gardening	maths	eggs	spinach

Example: Katrin lives in Munich. She comes from Germany and speaks German and English. She plays table tennis and collects stickers. She likes sweets and hates gardening.

5·4 A gentleman

What can you say about this gentleman? Write down sentences.

name	David	30	to be 30 years old
to live in	London	GB	to come from
to live in	flat	4 rooms	to have 4 rooms
to work as a	teacher	big school	to work in a
to speak	English	German	to speak
to be	married	2 children	to have
to like	football	Italy	
	fishing	boxing	
		TV	to hate
to play	tennis	beer	
		warm milk	
to collect	stamps		
	records		

Example: His name is David. He is thirty years old.

5.5 General facts: The solar system

Reading

Read the following text and fill in the right words in the riddle below.

There are nine planets in our solar system. They all go round the sun. Our earth is one of the sun's planets. The earth goes round the sun once a year. At the same time it spins round and round on its own axis once in twenty-four hours. For the people on earth it seems as if the sun rises in the east and sets in the west.

Some planets have satellites. A satellite goes round a planet. The earth has one satellite. It's the moon. The moon goes round the earth once in twenty-eight days.

to spin – um sich drehen
axis – Achse

to rise – aufgehen
to set – untergehen

Grammar

Signalwörter

Folgende Signalwörter zeigen dir an, dass du *simple present tense* verwenden musst:

1. Für Tätigkeiten und Vorgänge, die sich wiederholen oder immer wieder passieren:

often	oft	*every day*	jeden Tag
always	immer	*never*	niemals
sometimes	manchmal	*usually*	gewöhnlich
seldom	selten		

2. Für Handlungen, die aufeinander folgen:

first	zuerst	*lastly*	zum Schluss
then	dann	*finally*	zum Schluss
after that	danach		

5.6 What do you do?

Write sentences about the children and about yourself.

	Fred	Daniele	Peter	You
listen to CDs	sometimes with friends	never on Mondays	every day	
read books	often	sometimes	seldom	
play football	often	never	never	
do house-work	never	seldom	every day	
watch TV	usually in the evening	sometimes pop shows	often action movies	

Example: Fred sometimes listens to CDs with friends.

Continue in your exercise book.

5.7 Jobs at home

Look at the pictures and write down in your exercise book what Fred does at home.

do the cooking – wash the dishes – clean the floor – do the shopping – wash the car – set the table – water the flowers – clean the shoes – make breakfast – empty the dustbin – make the beds – wash the clothes – tidy the bedroom

Examples:

Fred waters the flowers.
Fred does the cooking.
...

5.8 Over to you: Family jobs

Write down in your exercise book how often you and the members of your family do these jobs.

I	never	do(es)	the cooking
My	sometimes		the washing-up
– mother	often		the shopping
– father	usually	wash(es)	the car
– brother	seldom	lay(s)	the table
– sister	always	clean(s)	the shoes
		repair(s)	broken things

5.9 Waking up in the morning

Write down how Fred wakes the boy up. Write in your exercise book. Use the following signal words:

first – then – after that – finally

This list will help you:

to offer – anbieten
to pour – gießen / strömen
hole – Loch

offer sausage – hen lay an egg – sleeping boy wake up – wag tail – make hole in fish tank– bell ring – egg fall into net – water pour down – gun fire

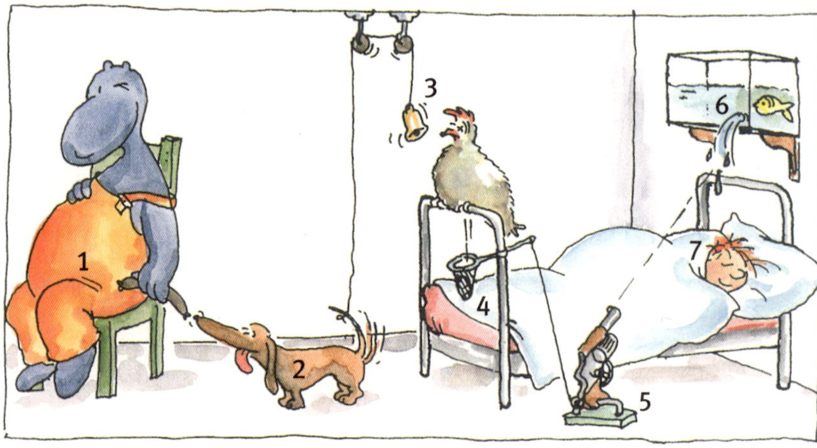

Example: First Fred offers a sausage to his dog.

5.10 Getting up in the morning

What does Fred do every morning? Match the morning activities to the pictures and write them down in the right order.

to stretch – strecken
towel – Handtuch

Every morning Fred gets up at seven o'clock [1]. Then Fred goes into the bathroom ☐. Then he has a shower ☐. He washes his hands and his face ☐. Fred stretches his arms ☐. He gets out of bed ☐. After that he dries his body with a towel ☐. He puts on his shirts and his pants ☐. He rubs his eyes ☐. Finally Fred leaves the house and goes to the bus stop ☐. Then he goes downstairs to the kitchen ☐. There he sits down at the breakfast table and has breakfast ☐.

Simple Present – Present Progressive

Neben dem *simple present* hast du bereits das *present progressive* kennen gelernt. Hier findest du eine Gegenüberstellung der beiden Zeiten.

Grammar

	Simple Present	Present Progressive
Bildung	Personalpronomen **und** Verb in Grundform, in der 3. Person Singular kommt ein **s** an das Verb: ***I sing.*** ***He sings.***	Personalpronomen **und** eine Form von ***to be (am, is, are)*** **und** die Endung **-ing** ***I am singing.*** ***He is singing.***
Verwendung	– wenn etwas wiederholt wird oder immer passiert – wenn etwas immer so ist – wenn Handlungen aufeinander folgen	wenn eine Handlung gerade passiert
Signalwörter	Für Tätigkeiten und Vorgänge, die sich wiederholen oder immer wieder passieren: *often, always, sometimes, seldom, every day,* Für Handlungen, die aufeinander folgen: *first, then, after that, lastly, finally*	*look, listen, just, just now, at the moment*

5.11 Simple present or present progressive?

Fill in the verb in the correct tense.

1. Look! It .... (begin) to rain.
2. We .... (have) English now.
3. Mr. Evans .... (laugh) very much.
4. The bus always .... (stop) at this corner.
5. We .... (have) English four times a week.
6. It is 8 o' clock. The bus .... (come).

Reading

5.12 A fairy tale

Lies das Märchen sorgfältig durch, denn wir stellen dir einige Aufgaben dazu.

Cinderella

evil – böse
stepmother – Stiefmutter
ugly – hässlich

Cinderella has no mother. She lives with her evil stepmother and two evil stepsisters. Her sisters hate her because Cinderella is a beautiful girl and they are very ugly. Cinderella has to do all the work in the house. Her sisters don't help her.
One day the prince holds a big ball at his castle. The ugly sisters are going to the ball. Cinderella has to help them put on their beautiful dresses. Cinderella can't go to the ball. She has got no dress and no shoes. She is very unhappy and starts to cry bitterly.

fairy – Fee
to appear – erscheinen

Suddenly a good fairy appears. She says, "Don't cry, Cinderella! Do you want to go to the ball?"
"I'd like to go," says Cinderella, "but I can't. I have got no dress and no shoes." "I'll help you," says the fairy.

silk – Seide / seiden
coach – Kutsche

"Of course you can go to the ball. Here is a beautiful dress and a pair of shoes made of silk."
Then a coach with six horses takes her to the castle. But she has to be back home by midnight.
Cinderella is very happy. She meets the prince at the ball. They dance and dance all night. The prince falls in love with Cinderella because she is so beautiful. But then midnight comes and Cinderella has to run home. She runs away but she loses one of her shoes. The prince runs after her but he can't see her. Then he finds her shoe.
The next morning he calls his men and tells them, "Go into every house in town. Find that beautiful girl for me!" And he gives them the silk shoe. The men go into every house. Every girl tries the shoe on, but it doesn't fit. They come to Cinderella's house. Her sisters try the shoe on, but it doesn't fit.
Then Cinderella comes. She puts on the shoe and it fits. Her sisters are very angry. "You are the girl," the men say and bring her to the castle. The prince is very happy to see Cinderella. "Will you marry me?" he asks.

to marry – heiraten

"Yes, I will," says Cinderella. The prince marries her and they live happily ever after.

6.2 Questions with *does*

Ask questions and answer them.

1. Peter likes sport.
   Does .... he play football?
   Yes, he does.

2. Jacko is a monkey. ....
   he eat bananas? ....
3. Mrs. Black is a pilot. ....
   she fly planes? ....
4. Brenda is a pupil. .... she go to school? ....
5. John helps his mother in the kitchen. .... wash the dishes?
   ....

6.3 Mixed questions

***Ask questions with* do / does.**

1. The cat likes fish.
   Does the cat like fish?

2. You speak English.
   ....
3. Peter rides his bike.
   ....
4. I know my headmaster.
   ....
5. You often go to the cinema. ....
6. Teachers mark tests. ....
7. The pilot flies planes. ....
8. We play tennis every summer. ....
9. Children like sweets. ....
10. She lives on the second floor. ....
11. Fred likes dogs. ....

6.4 Mixed exercise

Ask questions and mark with a cross.

		Do	Does	Question
1.	Mary gets up at a quarter to seven.	☐	☒	Does Mary get up at a quarter to seven?
2.	She goes to the bathroom.	☐	☒	Does she
3.	Her mother makes her breakfast.	☐	☐	
4.	Her father and Jimmy come down from the bedroom.	☐	☐	
5.	The dog barks in the garden.	☐	☐	
6.	Jimmy opens the door and goes into the garden.	☐	☐	
7.	Peter, Brenda and Susan wait at the gate.	☐	☐	
8.	They all go to school.	☐	☐	
9.	It snows in winter.	☐	☐	
10.	Jack remembers him.	☐	☐	
11.	He speaks English very clearly.	☐	☐	
12.	John laughs a lot.	☐	☐	
13.	We come to class on time.	☐	☐	
14.	Your father plays football.	☐	☐	
15.	I wash my face every morning.	☐	☐	

to remember – erinnern

Verneinung mit *to do*

Sätze, in denen **weder** eine Form von ***to be*** **noch** ein **Hilfsverb** vorkommen, bilden die **Verneinung** mit der Umschreibung **durch** ***to do***. Die Verneinung wird wie bei *to be* und *have got* mit ***not*** gebildet. Auch hier gibt es Kurzformen: ***do not*** wird zu ***don't***, ***does not*** zu ***doesn't***.

	Subjekt	Prädikat	Objekt
Aussagesatz:	*Tom and Kevin*	*like*	*ice cream.*
Verneinung:	*Maria and Brenda*	*do not (don't) like*	*ice cream.*

Wie bei der umschriebenen Frage wandert auch bei der Verneinung das **-s** des Verbs bei der 3. Person Singular zum ***do***. Es wird dann zu ***does***.

Example:
Tom likes potatoes.
Verneinung: *Tom does not (doesn't) like potatoes.*

Grammar

Bilde **nie** die **Verneinung** eines Satzes einfach mit *not*, **ohne** ein **Hilfsverb** oder ***to do*** zu verwenden.

6.5 Likes and dislikes – eating and drinking

Write down sentences in your exercise book.

Example: I like juice but I don't like milk.

biscuits juice potatoes toast tomatoes

meat onions carrots chocolate rice

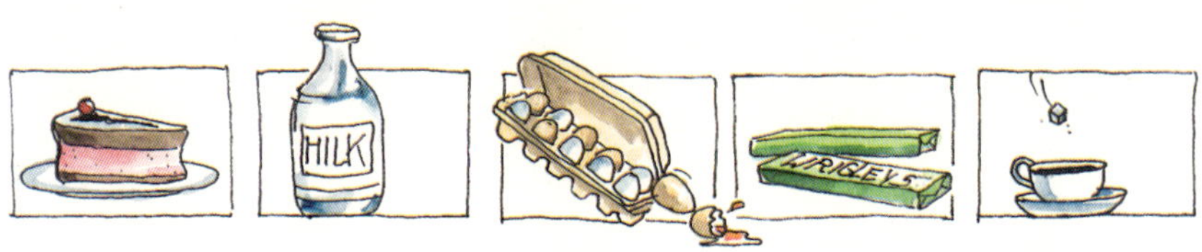

cake milk eggs chewing gum coffee

bread water jam lemonade bacon

6.6 The likes and dislikes of Mr. Brown

Complete the sentences. Use the phrases below.

work – doing the washing-up – going to work – driving the car – listening to music – going out for walks – cleaning the car – drinking beer – reading the newspaper – drinking tea

+

Mr. Brown likes drinking beer but he doesn't like drinking tea.

−

+

Mr. Brown likes ....

....

−

+

....

....

−

+

....

....

−

+

....

....

−

6.7 Billy and Brenda are talking about school

***Fill in* do/does, don't.**

Billy: .... you like to go to school?

Brenda: Yes, I do.

Billy: .... learn English at school?

Brenda: No, ...

Brenda: .... your teacher speak German?

Billy: Yes, he ....

Billy: .... your teacher drink milk during the lesson?

Brenda: No, ...

Brenda: .... your teacher read a newspaper during lesson?

Billy: ...., he ....

Billy: .... your parents help you with your homework?

Brenda: Yes, ...

Billy: .... you and your friends like geography?

Brenda: No, ...

6.8 Over to you: Dos and don'ts

What do you do and what don't you do? Write down the answers in your exercise book.

Do you live with your parents?	Do you play tennis?	Do you often go swimming in summer?	Do you know how to dance?
Do you often watch television?	Do your friends often play games with you?	Do you like school?	Do you walk to school every day?
Do you like watching football games?	Do you go to school by bus?	Do you like maths?	Do you do your homework in the afternoon?
Do you do your homework in the evening?	Do you like pets?	Do you collect stamps?	Do you sometimes go to pop concerts?
Do you sometimes go to discos?	Do your friends often ride their bikes?	Do you like going shopping?	Do you buy sweets with your pocket money?
Do you get money if you help your par-ents?	Do you get enough pocket money?	Do you sometimes get money as a present?	Do you buy clothes with your pocket money?
Do you have any brothers or sisters?	Do you live in a house?	Do you live in town?	

7. Parts of the Body

Words

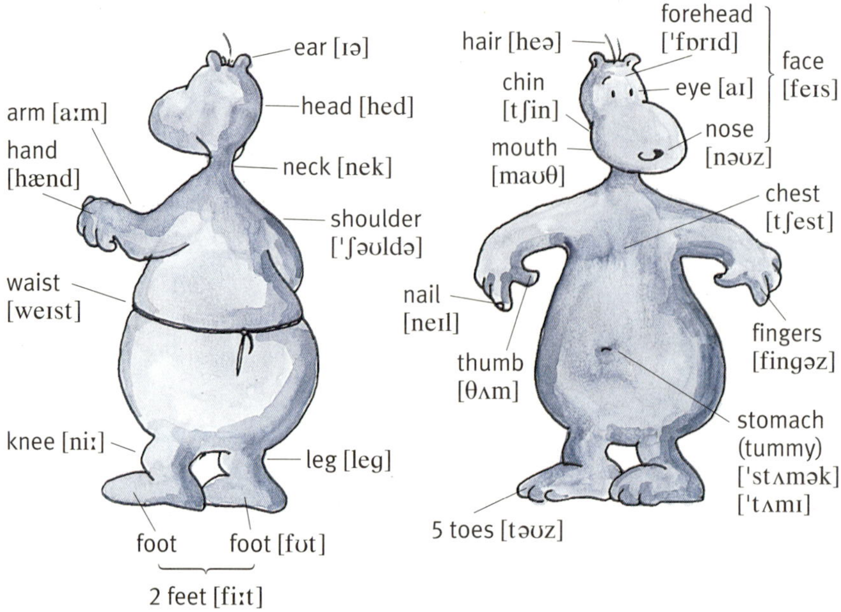

7.1 What is it?

Fill in the gaps.

1.  It's on your neck. It's your ....

2.  You can smell with it. It's your ....

3.  You can speak with it. It's your ....

4.  You can hear with them. They're your ....

5.  Its colour can be brown, grey, black, red or fair. It's your ....

6.  You have five .... on each ....

7.  You have one .... on each ....

8.  You can see with them. They're your ....

7.2 Mixed exercise

Put the right word into the gap.

1. The little boy rides on his father's shoulders .... (shoulders / ~~nose~~)
2. The neck is between the .... and the .... (chest / hands / ears / head)
3. The girl with the long .... runs very fast. (toes / legs)
4. Little Brenda has eaten too much cake, now her .... hurts. (leg / tummy)
5. Our neighbour wears a hat on his .... (ears / head)
6. The old gentleman has grey .... (knees / hair)
7. The teacher says, "Put your .... up." (hand / face)
8. It's wintertime and cold. Sarah runs home. She has a red .... (tummy / nose)
9. Karen has very good .... She hears very well. (feet / ears)
10. Wash your .... before you eat. (hair / hands)
11. Tom has good .... He can see the little bird. (toes / eyes)
12. Jessica plays the guitar with her .... (fingers / feet)

neighbour – Nachbar

7.3 What can you do with what?

Choose the right words from the list.

with your mouth you can

call
__at
d___k
___ea__
___gh
sm___
ki__
ta__k

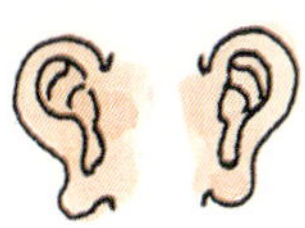

with your ears you can hear and listen to your

s__n__s
w___s
m___c
te____r

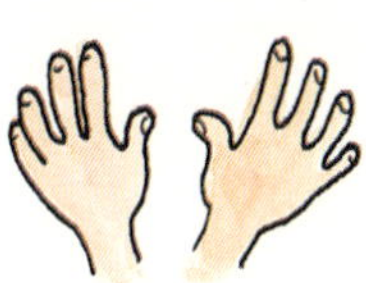

with your hands you can

w____
__arr__
l__t
__oi___
d___w

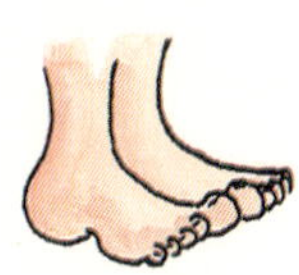

with your legs and feet you can

w__k
d___e
__u___
__um__
__t___d
r__n
h___y

eat – carry – dance – music – point – walk – laugh – draw – kiss – speak – rush – words – write – drink – teacher – sounds – run – smile – hurry – jump – call – lift – stand – talk

7·4 An alien

Arrange the letters of the words below in the right order and fill in.

1. cenk	2. hdna	3. ofot	4. nich	5. eekn	6. are	7. grefin	8. eto
9. eons	10. toumh	11. adeh	12. egl	13. roleduhs	14. tsech		
15. machost	16. raih	17. bumth	18. yee	19. daeehorf			

7·5 Monsters

Match the monsters with their descriptions. Fill in the matching numbers.

This monster is very big. It's got a round head with five eyes, two noses and one mouth. It's got three arms, six hands with three fingers each, four legs and four big feet. ◯

This monster has got three eyes, three noses and two mouths. It's got two arms and two hands with four fingers each. It's got six legs. ◯

This monster is big and fat. It's got four arms, very big hands, three very long legs and small knees. It's got four big eyes and six ears. It's got a big mouth with sharp teeth. ◯

Words

How to describe a person

face		eyes (colour)	eyes (type)
round	glasses	blue	large
square	beard, moustache	brown	small
		black	
		green	
		hazel	

hair (colour)	hair (type)	
red	curly/wavy	fringe
brown	straight	pony-tail
blond	bald (no hair)	
black		
grey		
fair/dark		

nose	mouth	ears
large/big	small	large
small	wide	small
straight	full lips	round
	thin/narrow lips	close to head

height			build		
tall	medium size	short	thin	big/solid	plump/fat

moustache [mə'sta:ʃ] – Schnurrbart
square – quadratisch

fringe – Pony

height – Größe
build – Körperbau

solid – untersetzt

7·6 Matching exercise

Match the numbers to the letters.

large nose	1
He's tall.	2
She's wearing glasses.	3
small nose	4
large eyes	5
grey hair	6
small mouth	7
small eyes	8
He's tall and fat.	9
a square face	10
ears close to head	11
She has a fringe.	12
straight nose	13

große Augen	A	breiter Mund	K	kleine Nase	U
rundes Gesicht	B	dunkles Haar	L	Er ist klein.	V
Schnurrbart	C	blondes Haar	M	kleine Ohren	W
Er ist groß u. dick.	D	dünne Lippen	N	kleine Augen	X
Sie trägt einen Pferdeschwanz.	E	Er hat einen Bart.	O	Sie hat einen Pony.	Y
Er ist mittelgroß.	F	eng anliegende Ohren	P	lockiges Haar	Z
quadratisches Gesicht	G	schmaler Mund	Q	Sie ist groß und dünn.	a
glatte Haare	H	Sie trägt eine Brille.	R	blaue Augen	b
Er ist groß.	I	gerade Nase	S	große Nase	c
volle Lippen	J	kahlköpfig	T	graues Haar	d

blue eyes	30
straight hair	29
He's got a beard.	28
full lips	27
dark hair	26
round face	25
wide mouth	24
thin lips	23
His head is bald.	22
moustache	21
He's of medium size.	20
She wears her hair in a ponytail.	19
curly hair	18

small ears	14	He's short.	15	She's tall and thin.	16	fair hair	17	curly hair	18

7·7 Funny faces

Here are three faces. Which one is Jack? Which one is Bill? Which one is Ned? Write the names under their pictures.

....

....

....

Bill has got long curly hair. His nose is small and short. His eyes are small, his mouth is narrow. He's got quite a long beard and a moustache.

Ned has got long straight hair. His nose is big and his mouth wide. His eyes are round and large.

Jack's got a square face. His nose is small and his mouth is narrow. He's nearly bald and wears glasses.

Dialogue

7.8 Play this game with a friend

Here are some more faces. Tell your friend about them. Don't say the person's name. See if your friend can guess which person you are thinking of.

Nick

Coco

Jojo

Edward

Aunt Mary

Elisabeth

7.9 Over to you: A description of yourself

Glue your photo here and describe yourself.

glue – kleben

This is me. My name is .... I think I am .... (too small, too tall, just right) because I am .... centimetres tall. My face is .... but .... My hair is .... My nose is .... and my ears are .... I am .... (quite happy / not happy) with my looks. My favourite colours are .... I mostly wear .... or ....

8. Clothes

Words

A fashion show

Weil eine Hose zwei Hosenbeine hat, gibt es das englische Wort ***trousers*** nur im Plural: *Your trousers are too tight*. Das gilt ebenso für ***jeans/shorts***. Eine Hose heißt: ***a pair of trousers***.

Reading

8.1 A puzzle game

Shorts and trousers

Tom, Dick and Jack are wearing shirts and trousers. Their shirts are red or blue. Their trousers are green or blue. Two boys are wearing green trousers. One boy is wearing a red shirt and green trousers. One boy is wearing a blue shirt and green trousers. One boy is wearing a red shirt and blue trousers. Jack and Tom are wearing red shirts. Dick is wearing green trousers.

What colour of shirt and trousers is Dick wearing?

8.2 What are they wearing?

Write the names of the clothes into the labels.

8.3 A clothes puzzle

Write the names of the clothes on the lines.

Clothes

1. tcao coat
2. sneja jeans
3. otobs ____
4. rusotrse ____
5. eit ____
6. koscs ____
7. lasdnas ____
8. retaews ____
9. gracdnia ____
10. ebluos ____
11. sehos ____
12. cjtkae ____

8.4 The clothes monster

Write the names in the grid.

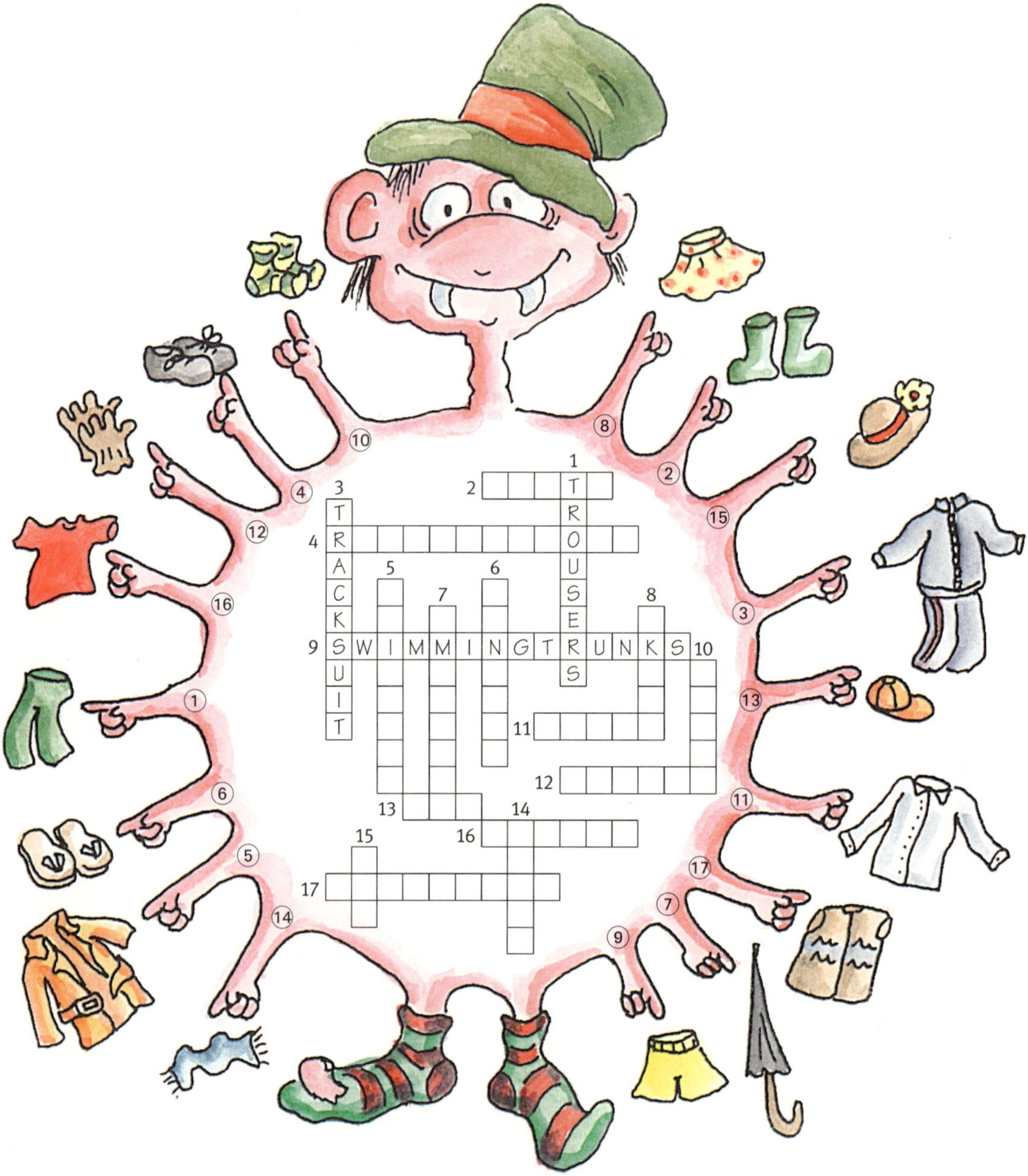

8.5 Roundabout

Write the names of the clothes on the lines. Find the clothes which sound the same as the things in the pictures. Draw lines.

Lies die Wörter auf dem äußeren Kreis laut vor. Schreibe dann die Namen der Kleidungsstücke auf und verbinde die Reimwörter.

Examples:
sky – tie
cat – hat

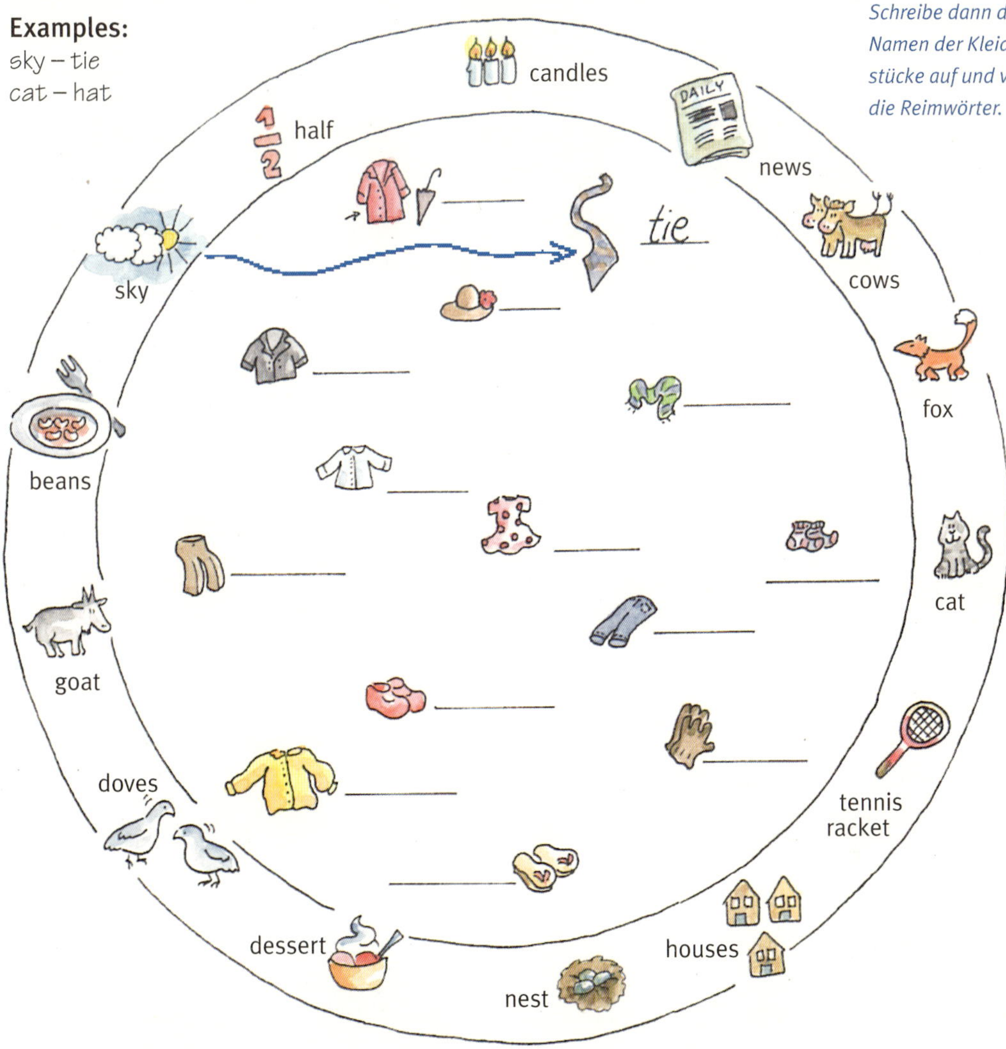

8.6 Over to you: What I wear

Answer the questions.

1. What do you wear on your hands? ....
2. What do you wear on your feet? ....
3. What do you wear on your head? ....
4. What do you wear when it rains? ....
5. What do you wear when it's cold? ....
6. What do you wear when it's warm? ....

Reading

8.7 Wolf! Wolf!

Read the song aloud and write the correct numbers of what the wolf is doing in the boxes.

Children:	We go to the park in the morning, When the wolf is still at home. Wolf! Wolf! What are you doing?
1. Wolf:	I'm putting on my trousers.
2. Wolf:	I'm putting on my shirt.
3. Wolf:	I'm putting on my shoes.
4. Wolf:	I'm putting on my sweater.
5. Wolf:	I'm putting on my jacket.
6. Wolf:	I'm putting on my hat.
7. Wolf:	I'm getting a plate.
8. Wolf:	I'm getting a fork.
9. Wolf:	I'm getting a knife.
Children:	What for?
10. Wolf:	To eat you!

Words

Describing clothes

Material

Woll ...

Seiden ...

Baumwoll ...

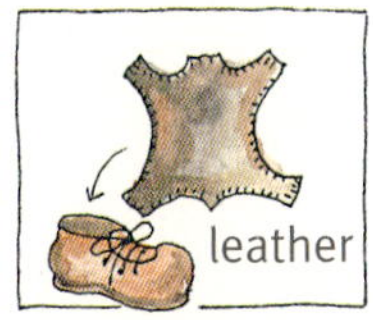

Leder

Looks

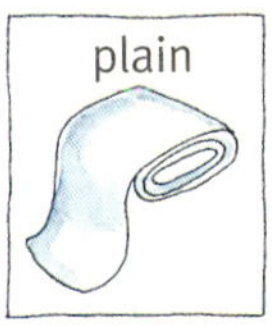

einfarbig

kariert

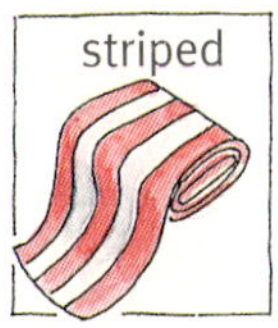

gestreift

gepunktet

gemustert

gut sitzend

kurz

weit

lang

eng

langärmlig

kurzärmlig

ohne Ärmel

übergroß

8.8 What can you see?

a flowered blouse

....

....

....

....

....

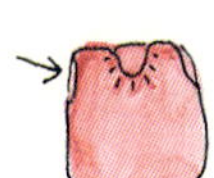

....

....

8.9 Clothes and colours

Read the text and colour the clothes.

Colour the striped suit blue, the plain skirt red, the sandals brown, the coat green, the spotted tie blue, the pair of jeans blue, the anorak grey, the gloves brown, the checked shirt pink, the shorts red, the striped scarf red and yellow, the socks brown, the cap red and white, the flowe-red blouse blue, the leather belt black, the cardigan yellow, the sleeve-less jumper orange, the shoes black, the T-shirt white, the boots yellow, the jacket brown, the flowered dress blue and yellow, the spotted skirt light yellow, the leather jacket black, the watch blue.

8.10 Describe Penny the punk

Write in your exercise book.

Hello! I'm Harold Brown. I'm with my sister Penelope, called Penny the punk. I'm wearing a yellow pullover, a black leather belt, a pair of striped trousers, grey spotted socks – (you can't see them) – and yellow and blue trainers. Penny is wearing a striped T-shirt, ...

Example:
Penny is wearing a striped T-shirt, ...

8.11 People and their clothes

Write the missing words in the blanks. Choose words from the list.

spotted – trousers – boots – belt – scarf – patterned – hat – skirt – belt – jeans – shirt – gloves – jacket – coat – leather – boots – striped – shirt – leather – sandals – striped – plain – jacket

Richard **Ted** **Peggy** **Mr. Rich** **Mrs. Adams**

Richard is wearing a pair of black ...., a pair of blue ...., a leather ...., a plain .... and a scarf round his neck.

Ted is wearing a brown leather .... and plain blue .... He is wearing a striped ...., a woollen .... and brown .... shoes.

Peggy looks beautiful in her .... dress with a black .... She is wearing a big .... on her head, nylon stockings and black ....

Mr. Rich is wearing a short ...., a .... waistcoat, a white .... and a .... tie. He is wearing .... on his hands and he is holding a stick.

Mrs. Adams is a businesswoman. She is wearing brown leather ...., a short ...., a big .... belt, a .... T-shirt and a .... jacket.

8.12 School uniforms

Info

In Großbritannien tragen die Schüler meist Schuluniformen.

This is what Jennifer and David say about their uniforms.

badge – Abzeichen

at least – zumindest

David:
We must wear a school cap, a white, blue or grey shirt and a tie with dark blue and light blue stripes. You can wear a black blazer with the school badge on it or a grey jumper. Then you must have black or grey trousers and any sort of shoes. My uniform costs nearly £ 250, because you have to have at least three shirts, two pairs of trousers and so on. That's a lot of money.

Jennifer:
The girls must wear a grey or black skirt, a white blouse and a cardigan or a blazer. Some have a tie, too. They must wear black shoes and white socks.

Write the names of the clothes on the lines.

Dialogue

8.13 Talk about what you wear at school

Write sentences.

We	have haven't	got a school uniform.

I	always sometimes never	wear	a hat a cap jeans a skirt a dress a blazer	to school.

9. Houses and Homes

Words

detached house

semi-detached houses

terraced houses

bungalow

church

factory

skyscraper

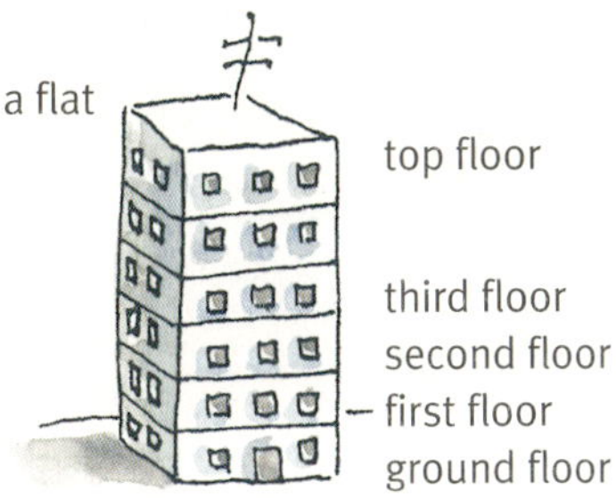

block of flats

flat – Wohnung

kennel

castle

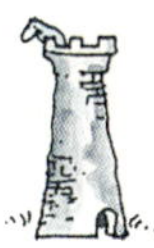
tower

farmhouse

cottage

treehouse

igloo

lighthouse

palace

9.1 There are many kinds of homes

Fill in.

You may live in a  .... in a town

or in a  .... in a big city

or in a  .... in the country.

You can also live in a  ....

Another kind of house is a  .... where

you may find a  ....

Here is an  .... His home is

an  ....

I have a  ...., his home is

a  ....

9.2 Over to you: Where I live

Describe your home. Make notes.

1. Do you live in a house or a flat? Yes, I do / No, I don't.
2. If it is a house, what kind of house is it? It's a ....

town-house – farmhouse – detached – semi-detached – terraced

3. If it is a flat, what is the building like? Which floor is your flat on? ....

....

a block of flats on the ground floor – on the ... floor

4. Have you got a garden? What is it like? ....

....

a large garden at the back of the house – no garden – a small garden – a garden where children can play

5. Does your house / flat have a balcony? What do you use it for? ....

....

hanging out the washing – growing pot plants – having meals in summer

Write sentences. Use your notes and write in your exercise book.

Today I want to tell you about ... where I live. ... is not far from .... It is .... There are .... Our ... has got ....

Words

A house

1. windows
2. roof
3. chimney
4. tree
5. garage
6. door
7. gate
8. grass
9. flowers
10. fence
11. smoke
12. wall
13. path

9.3 Colours

Colour this house.

The roof is red, the walls are yellow, the chimney is brown, the smoke is grey. The windows look silver. The door is blue. The grass is light green, the trees are dark green. The clouds are white, the sky is blue, the sun is orange. The garage is blue, the door of the garage is pink. The roof of the garage is red. The fence is brown, the gate is black. The path is brown.

9.4 What is what?

Fill in the blanks.

1. You enter the house by the ....
2. Smoke is coming out of the ....
3. You must go through the .... to get into the garden.
4. It's green, you can lie on it. It's ....
5. A house has got four ....
6. The car is in the ...., but you can't see it.
7. The .... is on top of the house and it is red.
8. Number one is ....
9. The .... is green and has got leaves.

Reading

9.5 Peter's house

Have a look at the drawing. Read the text and follow the description.

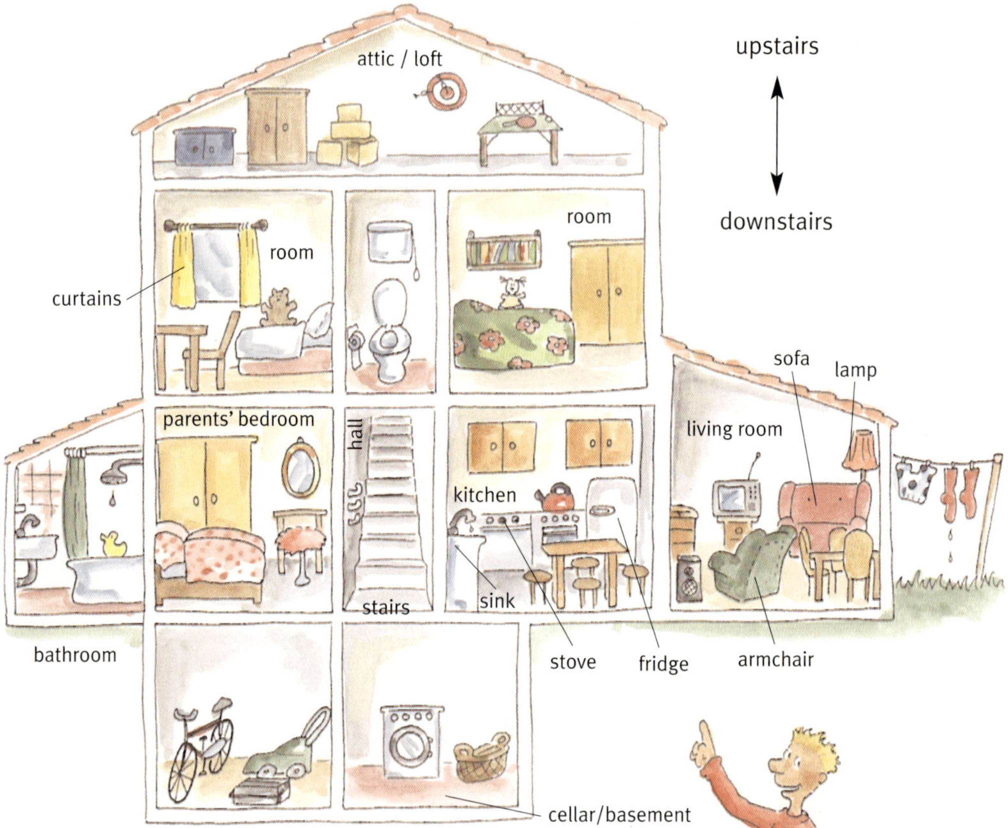

I live in a semi-detached house. I am very happy in our house, because I have a room of my own.

Our house has got two floors, a ground floor and a first floor. My room is on the first floor. From my window I can look into the street. I like to look out of the window and watch people passing our house.

pass – vorbeigehen

When you enter our house by the front door, you come into the hall. There are some pegs to hang the coats on. Stairs lead to the first floor.

important – wichtig

comfortable – bequem

On the ground floor is the living room, the bathroom, a kitchen and my parents' bedroom. The most important room on the ground floor is the living room, because the TV and my parents' stereo are in there. When my parents are out I like to sit on the comfortable sofa and listen to CDs or watch television.

The kitchen is small, but there's enough room for a table and four chairs, the electric stove, a dishwasher, the fridge and two cupboards.

On weekdays we have our meals in the kitchen, but on Sundays we eat in the living room.

In my parents' bedroom there is a big double bed, a dressing table with a mirror for my mother and a wardrobe for clothes. Sometimes I like to go into this room and lie down a little in the big double bed.

Upstairs there is my bedroom and my sister's bedroom. We have a small toilet.

Then there are stairs that lead up to the attic. It is full of cupboards and wardrobes and chests and boxes. In winter I can play table tennis or darts there. In summer it is mostly too warm under the roof.

We've got a cellar, too. We keep our garden things there, our bikes and our tools. A washing machine is down there, too. I sometimes help to carry the washing upstairs and to hang it on the line in our small back garden.

tool – Werkzeug

Answer the questions.

1. What kind of house does Peter live in? He lives in a ....
2. How many rooms are there altogether? ....
3. Why is Peter happy in his house? ....
4. What is the first room you get to after having entered the house? ....
5. Why is the living room very important for Peter? ....
6. Where do they have meals on weekdays? ....
7. What can Peter see from the window of his room? ....
8. Is there a room under the roof? If so, what is it called? ....
9. Where is the washing machine? ....
10. Is there a garden? ....

Reading

9.6 The old castle

Brenda, Sarah, Tim and Michael are describing the castle. Only one person is right. Who is it?

Tim
There's a big door in the middle and a small door on the left. There are lots of windows and there are two towers. It's got a big garden and there's a tree by the door.

Sarah
There are sixteen windows and there's a big door. The door's got a big round handle. There are two towers. It's got a garden and there's a river in front of the door.

Brenda
There's a river and a garden. There are three trees in the garden. There are lots of square windows and there's a round window at the top. The castle's got two towers.

Michael
The castle's got two doors and lots of windows. One window is round. There's a black gate and a bridge over a river. There are three trees in the garden.

Words

Things you do at home

play the guitar

play computer games

put on clothes

have a shower

do the washing-up

listen to music

have breakfast

cook

watch TV

read

brush your teeth

sleep

9·7 How many sentences can you write?

Choose a picture. Find the room. Write the sentence.

Example: 1. He does the washing-up in the kitchen.

9.8 Upstairs – downstairs

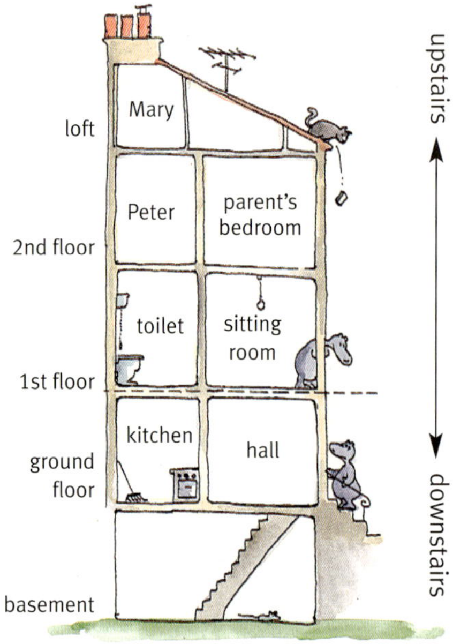

Say where the rooms are.

1. Peter's room is upstairs on the second floor.
2. The kitchen is downstairs ....
3. The parent's bedroom ....
4. The hall ....
5. The toilet ....
6. Mary's room ....

9.9 Over to you: What we do at home

Where do you and your family do what? Tick the boxes.

	in my room	in the kitchen	in the garden	in the bath-room	in the living room
I play with friends					
We eat					
I sleep					
We often sit					
We have breakfast					
I have my toys					
I listen to CDs					
We watch TV					
There are lots of pictures					
My favourite place is					

Now write a text in your exercise book about what you often do at home.

I sleep in .... We eat .... We have ....

Reading

9.10 Are you a good detective?

This room belongs to a girl. What do you know about her? What's her name?

Peggy	Carol	Lilly	Brenda
Peggy lives with her parents in a large house. She stays at home a lot. She likes watching TV. She hates cats but she has a dog. She likes to ride her bicycle. She always eats with her parents. She never cooks in her room.	Carol reads a lot. But she also likes sport. She likes to ride her bicycle and plays tennis. Her favourite animals are cats. She collects teapots. She's a student. She studies languages. She wants to be a translator. Her favourite food is chocolate, apples, peanuts and tomato soup.	Lilly loves sewing. She makes all her dresses. She never wears jeans. She eats a lot of chocolate. Her favourite singer is Michael Jackson. She is good at music. She plays the piano. Lilly also plays tennis and basketball. She works in a fruit shop but she never eats fruit. Her favourite drink is tea. She hates Coke.	Brenda plays the guitar and reads a lot. She always wears shirts or dresses. Coke is her favourite drink. She is a nurse and drives a car. She hates sport and she never rides a bicycle.

Notes

Before you decide, take down notes like these in your exercise book:

She plays tennis ... She ... jeans. She ... a bicycle. She watches ...
She collects ... She ... French and German. She often ... guitar.
She drinks ... She likes ...

Reading

9.11 The city quiz

Are you a "city person"? Find out by completing this questionnaire.

to complete – ausfüllen

to prefer – vorziehen

variety of shops – Auswahl an Läden

			Score
1.	Would you prefer to have	no garden?	6
		a small garden?	4
		a large garden?	2
2.	Would you prefere to live in	a flat?	6
		a small house?	4
		large house?	2
3.	Would you like working	indoors only?	6
		indoors and outdoors?	4
		outdoors only?	2
4.	Would you like working	with lots of people?	6
		in a small group?	4
		alone?	2
5.	Would you like to have	no pets?	6
		a cat?	4
		lots of animals?	2
6.	Do / Would you like to go	to a wide variety of shops?	6
		to a few different shops?	4
		to just one or two shops?	2
7.	Do / Would you like to eat	in restaurants?	6
		at friend's homes?	4
		at home?	2
8.	Do / Would you like to go to cinemas, theatres and concerts	often?	6
		sometimes?	4
		rarely (seldom)?	2

Score:

16–26: You are really a country lover.
You should be living in a village.

average – Durchschnitt

27–37: You are the "average" type.
You should be living in a town.

38–48: You are a "city person".
You should be living in a large city.

9.12 Time for a story

Reading

One night there is a heavy snowstorm, and in the morning Mr. Wilson's garden is full of deep snow. Mr. Wilson wants to take his car out, so he pays a man to clear the path from his garage to his gate. He says to the man, "Don't throw any snow on that side, because it will damage the bushes in my garden, and don't throw any on the other side, because it will break my fence. And don't throw any into the street, or the police will be angry." Then Mr. Wilson goes out.

to damage – beschädigen

When he comes back, the path is clear and there's no snow on the bushes, or the fence, or the street. Mr. Wilson is very happy – until he opens the garage to get his car out. The garage is full to the top with all the snow from the path and his car is somewhere under it all.

Answer the questions.

1. What happens one night? ....
2. What is Mr. Wilson's garden like in the morning? ....
3. What does he do then? ....
4. What does he say to the man? ....
5. What does he do then? ....
6. What does he see when he comes back? ....
7. How does he feel? ....
8. For how long does he feel like this? ....
9. What is the garage like? ....
10. Where is the car? ....

furniture – Möbelstück

10. Rooms and Furniture

Words

hall – Flur
floor – Fußboden!

The front door

1. letterbox 2. knocker 3. door
4. handle

The hall

1. peg 2. clock 3. stairs, staircase
4. key

The dining room

1. light 2. chair 3. table
4. trolley 5. cupboard

The study

1. curtains 2. shelf 3. globe
4. books 5. lamp 6. desk
7. chair 8. wastepaper basket
9. computer

The bedroom

1. mirror
2. lamp
3. pillow
4. wardrobe
5. double bed
6. alarm clock
7. dressing table
8. bedside table
9. duvet
10. stool
11. picture

stool – Hocker!
chair – Stuhl

The children's room

1. rug
2. toy
3. desk
4. stereo
5. satchel
6. poster
7. shelf
8. sofa
9. table

The kitchen

1. curtains 2. refrigerator/fridge
3. cupboard 4. bin 5. stool
6. dishwasher 7. sink

The sitting room

1. picture 2. table lamp
3. slippers 4. sofa, couch
5. armchair 6. bookshelves
7. carpet 8. TV set 9. cushion

The bathroom

1. window 2. toilet paper
3. rug 4. water tap 5. towel
6. bathtub 7. mirror 8. toilet
9. washbasin 10. shower

The basement

1. lawn mower 2. broom
3. sheet 4. saw
5. washing machine

10.1 A house crossword

Fill in.

10.2 A note

Here is a note for Frances. She is staying in the Evans' house while they are away on holiday. Fill in the words.

cats – cupboard – bedroom – blankets – bowl – dishwasher – door – key – kitchen – milk – shelf – sheets – stairs – towels – vacuum cleaner – water.

vacuum cleaner – Staubsauger

Dear Frances,

Here is a short note to say where things are in the house.
The .... and .... are in the .... at the top of the .... Extra .... are in the wardrobe in the small .... The .... is in the cupboard under the stairs. There's a back door .... on the .... above the .... in the .... One more thing. Could you feed the .... ? Also could you give them some .... in their .... outside the back .... every day? Don't give them ...., they don't like it.

Hope you have a good time.
Love, Mary.

10.3 Rooms and furniture

Write down the names of the rooms and furniture you can see.

1. bedroom
a) bedside table
b) w
c) d t

2. s
a) b
b) d
c) l

3. c r
a) b
b) c
c) p

4. b
a) b
b) w
c) m

5. s r
a) s
b) c
c) a

6. k
a) s
b) r
c) d

7. dining room
a) ch
b) c
c) l

8. cellar
a) w m
b) b
c) l m

10.4 What are the people doing in the house at the moment?

Write down which room the people are in and what they are doing.

1. Mrs. Taylor is in the kitchen. She is doing the washing-up.
2. Mr. Evans ....
3. Grandpa Ashing ....
4. Mr. Ashing and his friends ....
5. Fred and Fanny ....
6. Mrs. Evans ....
7. Mrs. Ashing ....
8. Mr. Taylor ....

to kiss – to play with the baby – to cook supper – to watch television – to drink wine – to have a bath – to do the washing-up – to look in the mirror

10.5 Brenda's dream room

Reading

This is a picture of my dream room. It is 15 metres long. In my dream room I have got a double bed and two armchairs. The bed has got a flowered blue and yellow cover, the armchairs are green.

The walls are a light yellow with blue stars. The carpet is red and white. There is a computer and a robot in my dream room. I've got two TVs, a CD player and a super hifi stereo.

There are shelves on the wall for my hundreds of books, magazines and comics.
My games and toys are in boxes on the floor beside my bed.
In my dream room there are a lot of pets.
Three cats, a big dog and two budgies.
The cats live in a basket, the dog sleeps under my bed and the budgies live in a cage.
My brothers and sisters are not allowed in my room and my mum and dad must knock at the door before they can come in.

Colour the picture of the room according to the text. Copy the table in your exercise book and write the things in the correct boxes.

furniture	pets	electronics	things to read and play with
bed	dog	computer	books

10.6 Over to you: This is my bedroom.

Choose the pieces of furniture from the lists below and draw a plan of your room in your exercise book.

1. rug
2. toy
3. desk
4. stereo
5. satchel
6. poster
7. shelf
8. sofa
9. table

1. curtains
2. shelf
3. globe
4. books
5. lamp
6. desk
7. chair
8. wastepaper basket
9. computer

Talk about your room. Write in your exercise book.

1. Do you have a room of your own or do you share a room?
2. Is it a big room?
3. Have you got a single bed, a double bed or a bunk bed?
4. Have you got a shelf?
5. Have you got any posters, pictures or photos?
6. What are your curtains like?
7. Have you got a carpet on the floor?

bunk bed – Stockbett

carpet – Teppich

11. The *there*-structure / Die *there*-Struktur

There is	no mirror in the kitchen.	Es gibt keinen Spiegel in der Küche.
	a TV set in the study.	Es gibt einen Fernseher im Arbeitszimmer.
	a sofa in the sitting room.	Es ist ein Sofa im Wohnzimmer.
There are	two beds in the bedroom.	Es gibt zwei Betten im Schlafzimmer.
	no posters in the bathroom.	Es sind keine Poster im Badezimmer.
	books on the shelf.	Es befinden sich Bücher im Regal.

Mit ***there is*** / ***there's*** oder ***there are*** kannst du Sätze beginnen, um auf das Vorhandensein von Dingen oder Personen hinzuweisen. Im Deutschen: es gibt, es ist, es sind, es befindet sich. ***There is*** (*short form* ***there's***) wird verwendet, wenn es sich um eine Person oder einen Gegenstand handelt. Bei mehreren Personen oder Dingen steht ***there are***.

Grammar

Question form
In der Frageform stellst du wieder um.

Predicate	Subject	
Is there	only one window in this room?	Yes, there is.
Are there	two doors in this room?	No, there aren't.
Is there	a new teacher in our school?	Yes, there is.
Are there	two new girls in our class?	No, there aren't.

In der Frageform wird – wie im Deutschen – Subjekt und Prädikat einfach vertauscht.

Grammar

11.1 What a funny house!

Schau dir das Bild an! Was stimmt nicht mit dem Haus?

bathtub – Badewanne

pig – Schwein

ceiling – Decke

Look at the picture and say what is wrong with the house.

1. There is .... a toilet upstairs in the sitting room.
2. There are .... stairs upstairs in the study.
3. There .... a bathtub downstairs in the children's bedroom.
4. There .... pigs downstairs in the ....
5. .... a coffee pot hanging from the ceiling.
6. .... clothes hanging on a line in the bedroom.

Now ask questions about the funny house and give the answers.

bookshelf – Bücherregal

7. Is there .... a bookshelf upstairs in the bathroom? Yes, there is ....
8. .... a shower upstairs in the sitting room? Yes, ...
9. .... pigs downstairs in the bedroom? No, there aren't.
10. .... books on the shelf? Yes, ...
11. .... a washing machine on the bed? Yes, ...
12. .... a TV set downstairs in the kitchen? No, ...
13. .... a boy sitting downstairs on the chair? No, ...

11.2 Stranger in a town

You want to know where some places are.

Du bist fremd in einer Stadt und willst wissen, wo die Orte sich befinden. Ordne zuerst die Namen den Bildern zu. Formuliere dann Fragen und Antworten.
– no
+ yes

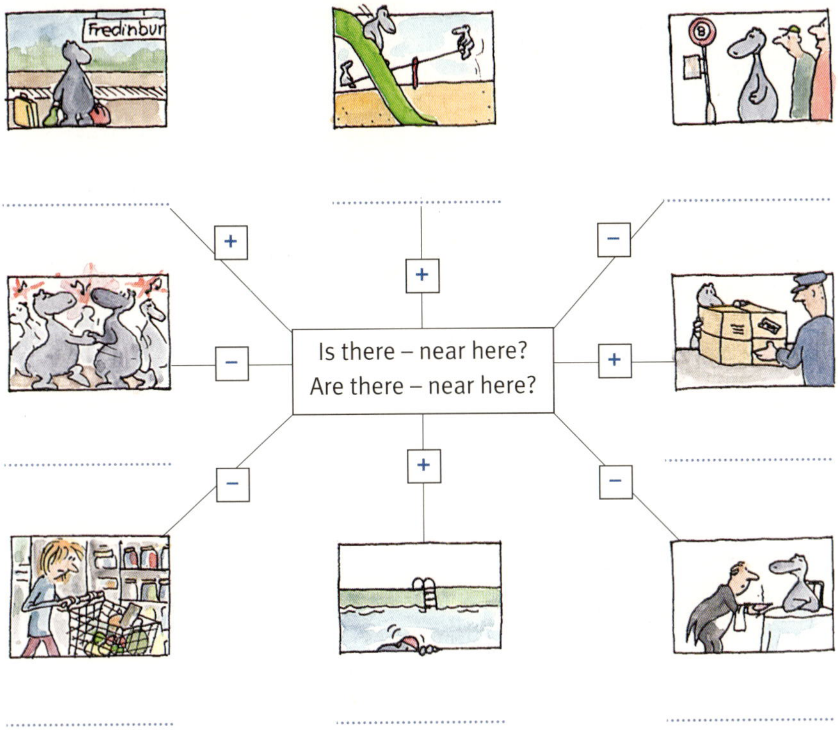

supermarket – post office – swimming pool – station – playground – bus stop – restaurant – discos

playground – Spielplatz

Example:

+ A: Excuse me, is there a swimming-pool near here?
  B: Yes, there is a very nice swimming pool over there.

− A: Excuse me, are there any discos near here?
  B: No, there are no discos near here.

+ A: Excuse me, ...?
  B: Yes, ...

− A: Excuse me, ...?
  B: No, ...

Continue in your exercise book.

12. Prepositions / Präpositionen

Grammar

Die verschiedenen Präpositionen

Präpositionen (Verhältniswörter) geben das Verhältnis von Personen, Dingen oder Sachverhalten zueinander an. Es gibt

1. ***Prepositions of place:*** Sie drücken aus, an welchem Ort sich jemand/etwas befindet (auf die Frage **wo**?).
2. ***Prepositions of movement:*** Sie drücken aus, in welche Richtung sich jemand/etwas bewegt (auf die Frage **wohin**? oder **woher**?).
3. ***Prepositions of time:*** Sie drücken aus, zu welcher Zeit oder in welchem Zeitraum sich etwas ereignet (auf die Frage **wann**?).

Prepositions of place – Ortsangaben

Where?

at – an

on – auf

under – unter

by/near – nahe

behind – hinter

beside – neben

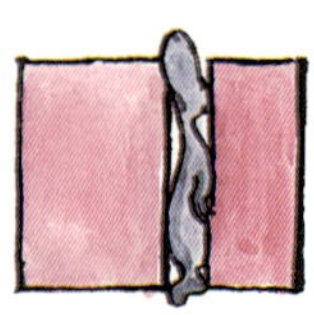
between – zwischen

in front of – vor, gegenüber

on the left – links

on the right – rechts

in/inside – in

opposite – gegenüber

over – über

above – oberhalb

below – unterhalb

next to – neben

round – um

among – unter

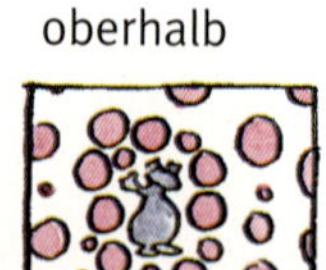
in the middle of – in der Mitte von

12.1 In front of / behind / on / under / between

The children are playing hide and seek. Where are they?

1. Brenda is standing in front of the garage door. She is looking for her friends. 2. Brian is sitting .... the table. 3. Anne is hiding .... the tree. 4. Tony is lying .... the roof of the garage. 5. Jenny is hiding .... the house. 6. The dog is sitting .... the chair.

12.2 A circus parade

Fill in the prepositions.

1. The monkey is walking behind the giraffe.
2. The elephant is walking .... of the zebra.
3. The zebra is walking .... the elephant and the giraffe.
4. The lion is walking .... the clown.
5. The clown is walking .... the horse.
6. The bear is at the end.
7. The camel is walking .... the monkey and the horse.
8. The lion is walking .... of the bear.
9. The giraffe is walking .... the monkey and the zebra.
10. The horse is walking .... the camel.

thief – Dieb

12.3 The thief

Number the sentences in the correct order. Then write them in your exercise book.

- ☐ Peggy is standing near the sitting room table now and looking for the recorder.
- ☐ She is lying on the sofa and crying.
- 1 Peggy is sitting at her desk doing her homework.
- ☐ She is standing opposite the hall door and telephoning the police.
- ☐ Now he is in the sitting room. He is taking the recorder.
- ☐ A man is standing at the window. He is looking at the cassette recorder.

12.4 Where are they?

Fill in the correct prepositions.

The girl is sitting .... on .... the chair.
(behind, on, by, under)

The boy is standing .... the trees.
(beside, next to, between, in front of)

Tony is hiding .... the door.
(before, at, behind, in front of)

The oranges are .... the box.
(into, in, on, out of)

The car is waiting .... the house.
(beside, in the middle of, in, in front of)

The dog is lying .... the car.
(above, under, near, at)

Prepositions of movement – Richtungsangaben

Grammar

Where to? Where from?

up – hinauf

down – hinunter

across – quer durch

over – über

round – um

along – entlang

after – hinter

towards – auf ... zu

from – von

through – durch

to – zu

against – gegen

out of – aus (... heraus)

into – in (... hinein)

about – hin und her

past – an ... vorbei

on to – auf (... hinauf)

12.5 What are the people doing?

Fill in the prepositions.

The pupils are running ....to.... school.
(out of, into, to)

The man is going .... the street.
(across, over, round, along)

Molly is running .... the stairs.
(over, down, up, above)

The dog is running .... the girls.
(against, into, through, after)

The boy is jumping .... the gate.
(about, on to, over, round)

The man is running .... the wall.
(out of, against, through, across)

Mr. Brown is going .... the house.
(from, past, on to, into)

12.6 The fly

Write down what the fly is doing.

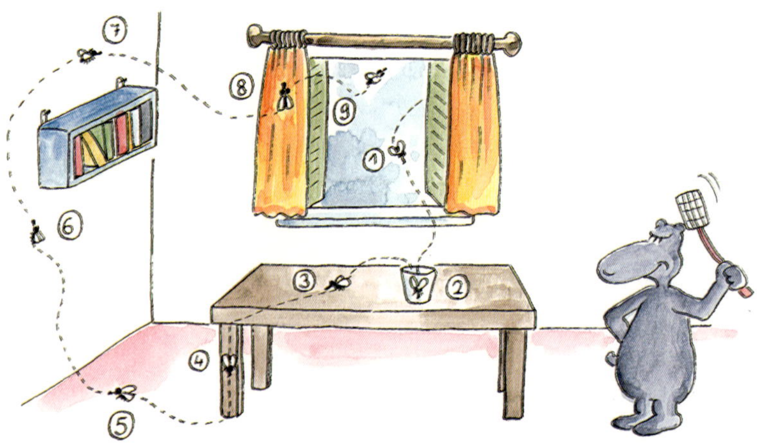

1. It is coming through .... the window. (come)
2. It .... the glass. (fly)
3. It .... the table. (sit)
4. Now it .... the table leg. (go)
5. Now it .... the floor. (walk)
6. It .... the wall. (climb)
7. Now it .... the bookshelf. (fly)
8. It .... the curtain. (climb)
9. At last it .... the window. (fly)

12.7 At the circus

Fill in the prepositions.

Let's talk about the picture! It is a circus. Can you see the big elephant? It is walking .... the circus ring. Try to find the horse which is running .... it. A clown is sitting .... a car. Another clown is falling .... There are three boys in the circus. They are riding bikes. One of them rides ...., one behind and one is .... them. Can you see the clown with the dog? The dog is running .... the clown. Can you see the two men flying .... the air? Two others are going .... and .... Two girls are standing .... their horses. They are riding .... a man. One clown is not in the circus ring. He is sitting with his back .... the wall.

12.8 A dream house

Fill in the prepositions.

1. The flowerpot is ......in...... the window.
2. Fred is looking .... the window.
3. The car is .... the garage.
4. The postman is going .... the path.
5. Fred is lying .... the grass.
6. Fred is .... the swimming pool.
7. The man is jumping .... the swimming pool.
8. The lady is lying .... the tree.
9. The men are sitting .... the table.
10. Mother is going .... the door.
11. The man is leaning .... the wall.
12. Smoke is coming .... the chimney.
13. The bird is sitting .... the roof.
14. The birds are flying .... the house.
15. The tree is .... the garage.
16. The tree is .... the house.
17. The dog is running .... the grass.
18. The cat is sitting .... the window.

13.2 This is Peggy's answer

Fill in the gaps.

15 Brixton Road
Streatham
London SW 3
10th October 20...

Dear Rainer,

Many thanks for your  .... It's in very good  .... I hope you and your family are well. We are all fine. Thank you, too, for the  .... and the German  .... You look very nice.

I haven't got a  .... but two  .... Their names are Jim and David. Jim is 16 .... now, and David is only 6 .... I am twelve years old. My home is in Streatham. It's in the south of London. We live in a  .... It only has three rooms, so I have to share my room with David.

I'm writing this letter on  .... It's  .... is here now. It's  .... a lot at the moment.

My hobbies are  ....,  ...., and  .... I also have a  ...., but my  .... are not very good.

We have two  .... A cat and a dog. They are very nice.

All the best,

From

Peggy

13.3 Over to you: Letter to a penfriend

Sender: ....

....

Date: ....

Dear ....,

Give your name (first name – surname): ....

Give your age: ....

Give information about where and how you live: ....

How many rooms your house/flat has got: ....

How many people live in it: ....

Write what your room looks like (furniture – colours etc.): ....

Give information about your school: ....

Write about your hobbies: ....

Find a good ending: ....

14. Phonetics

Da im Englischen leider nicht alle Wörter so ausgesprochen werden, wie man sie schreibt, hat man eine Lautschrift erfunden, die das Lesen und Aussprechen erleichtert. Diese Lautschrift ist auf der ganzen Welt gleich – und sie ist eine große Hilfe für dich, wenn du sie beherrschst.

Info

vowels – Selbstlaute, Vokale

Vowels		**Examples**	
[iː]	langes **i** wie in lieb – Stiel	*he – read – people – see*	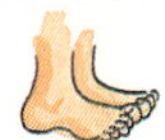 *feet*
[ɪ]	kurzes **i** wie in mit – bin – dick	*is – English – fit – kitchen*	 *ship*
[e]	kurzes **e** wie in Bett – Fett	*pet – friend – head*	 *pen*
[æ]	zwischen **ä** wie in Wäsche	*man – have – hand*	 *apple*
[ɑː]	langes **a** wie in baden – Vater	*dark – class – father – car*	 *arm*
[ɔː]	langes **o** wie in Mohr	*more – water – all*	 *door*
[uː]	langes **u** wie in Schuh – Schule	*who – blue – do – two*	 *moon*
[ʊ]	kurzes **u** wie in Buckel – Butter	*put – foot – look*	 *book*
[ʌ]	kurzes **a** wie in kann – matt	*but – come – mother*	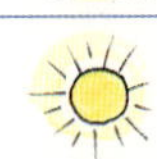 *sun*
[ə]	kurzes schwaches **e** wie in bitte – danke	*about – again*	 *banana*
[ɜː]	langes **ö** wie in fördern – aber länger	*word – bird*	 *girl*
[ɒ]	kurzes offenes **o** wie in Lotto – dort	*box – what – shop*	 *pot*

diphthongs – Doppellaute

Diphthongs		Examples	
[ɪə]	wie in Papier – hier	kommt im Englischen nur in der Verbindung des Vokals mit einem -r- vor *ear – here*	 *ear*
[eɪ]	keine Entsprechung	beide Buchstaben einzeln aussprechen, beginnt mit [e] endet mit [ɪ] *late – date – day*	 *pay*
[əʊ]	keine Entsprechung	aus der Stellung des schwachen [ə] gleitet die Zunge in die des [ʊ]-Lautes *go – no – know*	 *boat*
[aɪ]	wie Mai – Kaiser	*tie – nice – buy – eye*	 *pie*
[aʊ]	sauer – Haus	*down – round – now*	 *house*
[ɔɪ]	Leute – Beute	*toy – noise – voice*	 *boy*
[eə]	äh-Laut wie in Bär	kommt im Englischen nur in Verbindung des Vokals mit einem -r- vor *pair – there – where*	 *pear*
[ʊə]	keine Entsprechung	*poor – sure*	 *tour*

consonants – Mitlaute

Consonants		Examples	
[r]	nicht wie das deutsche r	Zungenspitze gegen Gaumen anheben und leicht zurückbiegen *rose – ring – front*	 *biro*
[s]	s wie in Laus – Kuss	stimmloses s *this – song*	 *horse*

Consonants		Examples	
[ŋ]	wie singen	*long – morning*	 *sing*
[w]	wie ein u vor dem w sprechen Quelle	*water – what – one*	 *way*
[v]	wie das deutsche w Winter – Vase	*very – village*	 *van*
[ʃ]	stimmloser sch-Laut wie Tasche – Busch	*dish – sugar – wish*	 *fish*
[tʃ]	t mit nachfolgendem Zischlaut wie klatschen	*teacher – cheap – much*	 *cheese*
[dʒ]	d mit nachfolgendem Zischlaut wie Dschungel	*jumbo – German – jet*	 *orange*
[ʒ]	stimmhafter sch-Laut wie Gelee	*television – pleasure*	 *television*
[θ]	keine Entsprechung	Zunge zwischen die Zähne, stimmlos lispeln *bath – thanks*	 *mouth*
[z]	stimmhaftes s wie summen – Nase	*is – boys – lazy*	 *rose*
[l]	dunkles l	*milk – wall – blue*	 *doll*
[ð]	keine Entsprechung	Zunge zwischen die Zähne, stimmhaft lispeln *that – weather*	 *mother*
[j]	wie j in jetzt	*yes – tube*	 *news*

14.1 Consonants

Lies die Wörter laut und höre dir gut zu.

Read aloud.

[v]	[w]	[s]	[z]
van	what	place	plays
very	window	sleep	noise
never	twelve	sister	nose
give	one	sit	girls

[ð]	[θ]	[r]	[ŋ]
this	thick	train	long
father	thin	rich	morning
that	through	room	hang
weather	think	very	riding

[ʃ]	[tʃ]	[dʒ]	[j]
fish	chair	age	yes
ship	much	German	tube
sharp	teacher	jeans	new
shop	watch	jumbo	queue

14.2 What can you see?

Ordne die Wörter den Dingen und Personen in den Bildern zu und lies die Wörter laut.

Write the words matching the pictures and read them aloud.

The sound [iː]

1. key
2. people
3. ....
4. ....
5. ....
6. ....
7. ....
8. ....

The sound [ɪə]

1. ear ....
2. ....
3. ....
4. ....
5. ....
6. ....

The sound [ɜː]

1. girl ....
2. ....
3. ....
4. ....
5. ....
6. ....
7. ....
8. hurt ....

The sound [eə]

1. chair ....
2. ....
3. ....
4. ....
5. ....
6. ....
7. ....

Reading

14.3 Funny rhymes

Read aloud.

[aɪ]

It's a fly
wearing a tie
holding a pie
and waving goodbye!

[æ]

It's a cat
sitting on a mat
wearing a hat
and watching a rat.

[aʊ]

A goat
sitting in a boat
wearing a coat
and writing a note!

[ɒ]

It's a cock
standing on a rock
wearing a sock
and looking at a clock!

[eə]

It's a bear
sitting on a chair
combing its hair
and holding a pear.

[iː]

A sailor goes to sea
to see what he can see
and all that he can see
is sea, sea and sea!

14.4 Words and pictures

Match the words to the pictures and read them aloud.

camp
man
baby
cap
eight
hat

milk
knife
pin
sign
mill
pig

snake
rain
gas
way
sad
play

who
bowl
pool
two
ghost
shoe

pet
ten
bee
desk
knee

fox
stocking
stop
foot
book
hot

like
pie
sky
girl
time

Put the words in the right bags.

Ordne die Wörter den richtigen Taschen zu.

[eɪ]	[æ]	[e]	[əʊ]	[ɜː]	[ɪ]	[aɪ]	[uː]	[iː]	[ɒ]	[ʊ]
baby	camp	pet	ghost	girl	pin	sign	shoe	knee	hot	foot

Textbook Rally

Schreibe die Zahlen alle aus.

Give the numbers in words.

1. Look at the beginning of the book. Count the pictures on page 7.
   There are ☐☐ ☐☐☐ pictures.
   26
2. How many units are there in the textbook?
   There are ☐☐☐ ☐☐☐☐ units.
   16 3
3. Go to page 13 and find out which month Fred's birthday is.
   Fred's birthday is in ☐ ☐☐☐.
   23
4. What is unit 4 about? It's about the ☐☐☐☐☐☐☐☐☐☐☐.
   1
5. Which unit is about clothes?
   It's unit ☐☐ ☐☐.
   24
6. How many Freds can you find on page 26? There are ☐☐ Freds.
   10

pronunciation – Aussprache

7. Sometimes the pronunciation of a new word is difficult. Where can you check English sounds?
   I can check English sounds starting on page ☐☐☐ ☐☐-☐☐☐☐☐.
   21
8. In unit 6 you learn about "do-questions". On which page are they explained?
   "Do-questions" are explained on page ☐☐☐☐☐ -☐☐ .
   9 25
9. Which fairy tale can you find in this book?
   ☐☐ ☐☐ ☐☐☐☐
   27 2
10. Which colour is the shoe in the fairy tale?
    The shoe is ☐☐☐ ☐.
    15 22
11. What is exercise 6.5 on page 45 about?
    It's about ☐☐☐☐☐ ☐☐ ☐☐☐☐☐☐☐.
    18 4
12. Go to pages 28/29. Find the stanza which talks about sandcastles and write down the month. It's ☐ ☐☐ ☐.
    11 5
13. On page 32 you get to know some European children.
    Who lives in Madrid? ☐☐☐☐ lives in Madrid.
    6
14. What does Katrin (p. 32) like?
    She likes ☐☐ ☐☐☐.
    17
15. Go to page 66. Does Peter have a room of his own?
    Yes/No
    7 7

16. Write down what Carol wants to be (page 71).
    She wants to be a □ □[13] □□□□□□□□.

17. What is Mr. Taylor doing on page 78?
    He is □□□□□□□ □[28] □[19] □.

18. What are Fred and Fanny doing on page 78?
    Fred and Fanny are □□ □[8] □□□ □ .

19. Go to page 85. What is the name of the first animal of exercise 12.2?
    It's a(n) □[14] □□□□ □[12] □□.

20. On page 94 you find a letter. What is Rainer's sister's name?
    Her name is □[20] □□□□□.

□□□□ □□□□:
1 2 3 4 5 6 7 8

"□□□ □□□ □□□□□!
9 10 11 12 13 14 15 16 17 18 19

□□□□ □□□□□!"
20 21 22 23 24 25 26 27 28

Lösungen

Lösungen Kapitel 1:

Seite 7 1.1

volleyball, radio, cowboy, jeans, bubble gum
baby, boots, clown, shop, sheriff
skatebord, hot dog, sandwich, (mountain) bike, colt / pistol
house, tent / camping, overall, (racing) car, walkman
girl, TV / television, plane / jet, boy, kiss
milk shake, swimming pool, T-shirt, horse, Fred

Seite 8 1.2

Sport: body building, inline skates, golf, volleyball, foul
Musik: cassette, jazz, music box, pop, song, oldie, hit, rock'n'roll
Essen / Trinken: bubble gum, cornflakes, drink, milk shake, hot dog, toast, steak, popcorn, sandwich
Freizeit / Vergnügen: camping, walkman, party, hobby, quiz, clown
Eigenschaften: fair, fit, down, out, clever
Kleidung: T-shirt, cotton, jeans, overall, shorts
Geschäftsleben / Berufe: boss, computer, manager, team, service, stewardess, job, babysitter
Fernsehen / Film: star, video, TV, show, story, killer, gangster
Verkehr / Straße / Stadt: jet, shop, jeep, supermarket, trip, highway, city, mountain bike, motel
Menschen: gentleman, boy, playboy, teenager, girl, lady, baby

Seite 9 1.3

Im Folgenden geben wir dir einige Mustersätze. Du kannst natürlich bei jedem Wort auch andere Sätze bilden.

like: I like ice cream.
two: I have got two brothers.
three: One plus two is three.
London: The capital of Great Britain is London.
can: I can play football.
colour: The colour of my hair is brown.
your: Is this your book?
fifteen: My brother is fifteen years old.
eighteen: I can go wherever I want when I am eighteen years old.
the: The book is green.
and: Six and eight is fourteen.
blue: My shirt is blue.
green: The grass is green.
yellow:The banana is yellow.
park: We go to the park on Sundays.
she: She is my sister.
cat: The cat is climbing a tree.
Coke: I would like a Coke, please.
banana: Bananas are fruit.
table tennis: I can play table tennis.
is: She is my sister.
her: Her dress is blue.
I: I am a boy.
Thursday: Thursday is a weekday.
seven: A week has seven days.
milk: I like milk.
old: I have got an old book.
car: Our car is very fast.
queen: The Queen is on TV on Christmas Day.
bed: I usually go to bed at nine p.m..
budgie: I have got a pet. It's a budgie.
on: The book is on the table.
crocodile: Crocodiles live in water.
water: The water is cold.
ice: Ice is slippery.
aunt: My aunt is very nice.
hamburger: Too many hamburgers are not good for me.
Goodbye: You say "goodbye" when you go home.

Lösungen Kapitel 2:

2.1 Seite 10

1. March	5. December	9. November
2. July	6. June	10. September
3. May	7. August	11. April
4. February	8. January	12. October

2.2 Seite 11

January / February / March / April / May / June / July / August / September / October / November / December

2.3 Seite 11

January is the first month of the year.
February is the second month of the year.
April is the fourth month of the year.
August is the eighth month of the year.
September is the ninth month of the year.
December is the twelfth month of the year.
May is the fifth month of the year.
November is the eleventh month of the year.
March is the third month of the year.

2.4 Seite 12

20.2. the twentieth of February / February 20th
1.1. the first of January / January 1st
30.3. the thirtieth of March / March 30th
3.11. the third of November / November 3rd
31.12. the thirty-first of December / December 31st
14.5. the fourteenth of May / May 14th
22.9. the twenty-second of September / September 22nd
9.7. the ninth of July / July 9th
5.4. the fifth of April / April 5th
8.8 the eighth of August / August 8th
2.6. the second of June / June 2nd

2.5 Seite 13

Dad's birthday is on the seventeenth of July.
Fred's birthday is on the first of April.
Aunt Mary's birthday is on the eighteenth of October.
Pam's birthday is on the twenty-sixth of January

2.6 Seite 13

Deine Lösung könnte ungefähr wie folgt lauten:
My birthday is on the eleventh of October. My mother's birthday is on the third of February. My father's birthday is on the first of January. I was born in 19..., my father was born in 19..., my mother in 19...

2.7 Seite 14

It's time to make my birthday wish.
What day's today? It's my birthday!
It's fun to bake a birthday cake.

Seite 14 **2.8**

Dear Claudia,
Many thanks for your letter. I hope you and your family are well. We are all fine.
I'm writing this letter on Sunday, the twenty-first of January. It's winter here now.
It's raining a lot at the moment. I can't cycle this weekend, so I'm staying at home listening to music, watching TV and writing this letter. Next Wednesday is my birthday and Mum is making me a big birthday cake. She's got eleven candles for it.
All my friends will come to my birthday party and we'll dance and sing. My birthday also means more pocket money.
Please write soon!
Best wishes
Michael

Seite 15 **2.10**

Deine Einladungskarte könnte ungefähr wie folgt lauten:
Dear Peter,
It's my birthday next Saturday. I'm going to have a party. The party is at 25 Regent Street. It starts at half past four p.m. Can you come? I hope so. See you on Saturday.
Lots of love
Alex

Seite 16 **2.11**

1. Susan's birthday is on the eleventh of October.
2. Susan is eleven years old.
3. In the morning Susan opens her birthday cards.
4. She gets seventeen cards from her family and friends.
5. She gets a new bike from her parents and a horse book from her brother. Her aunt gives her £ 25.
6. Susan's friends play a lot of games, dance and eat birthday cake.

Seite 16 **2.12**

Überlege, was du an deinem Geburtstag so alles tust. Bilde dann Sätze aus der "mindmap". Dein Text könnte wie folgt lauten:
On my birthday I invite my friends. We play games, dance or listen to music. Sometimes I go to the cinema with my friends.

Lösungen Kapitel 3:

Seite 17 **3.1**

1. sail	5. swim	9. skate
2. ride a bike	6. ride a horse	10. play football
3. dance	7. ski	11. fish
4. play tennis	8. climb trees	12. organise his stamps

Setze nun jeweils das Hilfsverb *can* vor das Verb und bilde Sätze.
He can ride a horse and a bike.
Fred can dance, sail, swim and skate.
He can ski and fish.
Fred can climb trees and organise his stamps.
Fred can play tennis.

Seite 18 **3.2**

Fred can't play the guitar with his broken arm.
He can eat with a spoon.
He can't use his computer.
Fred can't take a shower.
He can't do his homework.
Fred can go to bed.
He can't open bottles.
He can go to school.
He can't wash his ears.
He can't climb trees.

3.3 *Seite 19*

Hier kommt es darauf an inhaltlich sinnvolle Sätze zu bilden, z. B.:
Dogs can bark very loudly but they can't sing.
Budgies can sing very well but they can't smell very well.
Lions can climb trees but they can't sing.
Monkeys can eat bananas but they can't bark.
Horses can pull carts but they can't catch mice.
Snakes can live a long time without water but they can't jump.
Cats can catch mice but they can't fly.
Bears can swim but they can't sing.

3.4 *Seite 19*

B: I'm thinking of an animal.
A: Can it climb trees, Bob?
B: No, it can't.
A: Can it fly?
B: No, it can't.
A: Can it walk on two legs?
B: No, it can't.
A: Can it hear well?
B: Yes, it can.
A: Is it a lion?
B: No, it isn't.
A: Is it a dog?
B: Yes, it is.

3.5 *Seite 20*

Die Lösungen lauten von oben nach unten wie folgt:
Can you help me, please?
I can't see it very well.
Can you say that again, please?
I can't do this. It's too difficult.
Can you spell that word, please?
Can I open the window, please?
Can you show me your homework, please?
Can I write that word on the board, please?
Can you pronounce that word, please?
Achtung! Im Englischen musst du stets das Wort *please* bei einer höflichen Bitte gebrauchen.

3.6 *Seite 21*

2. Let's go sailing.
   Sorry, I can't. I must sweep the floor.
3. Let's go to the zoo.
   Sorry, I can't. I must do the washing-up.
4. Let's go to the football match.
   Sorry, I can't. I must do the cooking.
5. Let's go out.
   Sorry, I can't. I must do my homework.
6. Let's go swimming.
   Sorry, I can't. I must go shopping.
7. Let's go to the park.
   Sorry, I can't. I must clean the shoes.

3.7 *Seite 22*

Hier sind noch ein paar weitere Beispiele:
I can play football but I can't play an instrument.
I can write good stories but I can't draw clowns.
I can climb trees but I can't catch snakes.

3.8 *Seite 22*

Beantworte die Frage entweder nach der Vorgabe – wenn sie auf dich zutreffen – oder finde eigene Antworten. Zum Beispiel:
Can you go out whenever you want? Yes, I can but I have to ask my parents first.
What time do you have to be home? I have to be at home by seven o'clock.

Lösungen Kapitel 4:

Seite 24 4.2

1. It's winter.
2. It's summer.
3. It's autumn.
4. It's spring.

Seite 24 4.3

2. February begins at the end of January and goes on until the beginning of March.
3. Winter begins at the end of autumn and goes on until the beginning of spring.
4. Tuesday begins at the end of Monday and goes on until the beginning of Wednesday.
5. Summer begins at the end of spring and goes on until the beginning of autumn.
6. Sunday begins at the end of Saturday and goes on until the beginning of Monday.

Seite 25 4.4

I can only sunbathe during the summer.
I can only camp and swim during the summer.
I can only collect shells during the summer.

Seite 25 4.5

In summer the sun is warm. It's fun to camp near the sea. You can collect shells on the beach and swim in the water. If it's a cloudy day you can listen to music or read a book. Or you can walk in the park, cycle on your bike, and take photographs. You can sleep under the stars by the light of the moon.

Seite 26 4.6

Denke an Aktivitäten, die du im Winter machen kannst und bilde Sätze mit Hilfe der Wörter aus dem Winterbild. Hier sind noch zwei weitere Beispiele:
In winter I often go skiing with my parents.
Ice-skating is my favourite winter activity.

Seite 26 4.7

Winter is the best time of the year because in winter you can go skiing. I also like the long evenings when you can watch telly and read a lot of books. But the best part of winter is Christmas because on Christmas Eve I get a lot of presents from my parents and from my sisters and brothers. If there is snow I go into the garden and build a snowman. I am sure that wintertime is the best time of the year.

Seite 27 4.8

SUMMER
weather: warm, hot, sunshine
holidays: summer holidays
things: shorts, sea, birds, fish, leaves, boat, ice cream, beach
activities: camping, sunbathing, climbing, cycling, travelling, playing hockey, collecting shells, riding, swimming

WINTER
weather: cold, cool, snow, snowstorm
holidays: New Year, Christmas
things: snowman, white mountains, sledge, ski boots, ski sticks, scarf, cap, snowdrops
activities: skiing, having snowball fights, ice-skating

Lösungen Kapitel 5:

5.1 *Seite 30*

1. Harry's parents get up at seven o'clock every day.
2. They all have breakfast in the kitchen.
3. He goes to school by bus.
4. They live in the country.
5. Harry's mother is a teacher
6. They come home at four 'o clock.
7. In the afternoon Harry often plays football with his friends.
8. He listens to pop music.
9. He likes pop music.
10. In the evening they watch television.

5.2 *Seite 31*

2. it flies   3. she gets   4. he fetches   5. it does   6. she buys   7. it catches
8. he cooks   9. she hurries   10. he goes   11. she kisses

5.3 *Seite 32*

Halte dich bei Mustafa, Sven und Paula einfach an das Beispiel.

5.4 *Seite 32*

His name is David. He is thirty years old. He comes from Great Britain and lives in London. He lives in a flat which has four rooms. He works in a big school as a teacher. He speaks English and German. He is married and has two children. He likes football, fishing and travelling to Italy. He hates boxing, watching TV, beer and warm milk. In his spare time he plays tennis and he collects stamps and records.

5.5 *Seite 33*

The earth goes round the sun once a year. The moon goes round the earth once a month. The earth spins on its axis once a day.

5.6 *Seite 34*

Fred sometimes listens to CDs with friends. He often reads books. Fred often plays football in the school team and he never does housework. He usually watches TV in the evening.
Daniele never listens to CDs on Mondays. He never plays football but sometimes he reads books. He seldom helps with the housework and sometimes he watches pop shows on TV.
Peter listens to CDs every day. He seldom reads books and never plays football. Every day he does housework and he often likes watching action movies on TV.

5.7 *Seite 35*

3. Fred washes the clothes.
4. Fred empties the dustbin.
5. Fred cleans the floor.
6. Fred cleans the shoes.
7. Fred sets the table.
8. Fred washes the dishes.
9. Fred makes the beds.
10. Fred makes breakfast.
11. Fred tidies the room.
12. Fred washes the car.
13. Fred does the shopping.

Seite 35 **5.8**

Denke an deine Familie und überlege, wie häufig du und der Rest der Familie welche Aufgaben im Haushalt erledigen. Zum Beispiel:
I often lay the table and sometimes I do the washing-up. I never repair broken things. My father always repairs broken things and washes the car. He sometimes cleans the shoes. My mother usually does the cooking and she often does the shopping. My brother never does the cooking, the washing-up or the shopping. He never lays the table or cleans the shoes, and he never repairs broken things. He is too small. He is just three years old. But he is nice and I like him very much.

Seite 36 **5.9**

The dog wags its tail. Then the bell rings. The hen lays an egg. The egg falls into a net. After that the gun fires. It makes a hole in the fishtank. Then the water pours down. Finally the sleeping boy wakes up.

Seite 36 **5.10**

Fred stretches his arms. He rubs his eyes and gets out of bed. Then Fred goes into the bathroom. He washes his hands and his face. Then he has a shower. After that he dries his body with a towel. He puts on his shirt and his pants. Then he goes downstairs to the kitchen. There he sits down at the breakfast table and has breakfast. Finally Fred leaves the house and goes to the bus stop.

Seite 37 **5.11**

1. Look! It is beginning to rain.
2. We are having English now.
3. Mr. Evans laughs very much.
4. The bus always stops at this corner.
5. We have English four times a week.
6. It's 8 o'clock. The bus is coming.

Seite 39 **5.13**

1. true	8. false	15. true	22. false
2. false	9. true	16. false	23. true
3. false	10. false	17. false	24. false
4. true	11. false	18. true	25. true
5. false	12. true	19. false	26. true
6. false	13. false	20. false	
7. true	14. true	21. false	

Die Korrekturen der falschen Aussagen lauten:

2. Cinderella has two stepsisters.
3. Her sisters don't help in the house.
5. Cinderella's sisters go to the ball.
6. Cinderella hasn't got any dress or shoes.
8. The prince holds a ball, not the king.
10. The fairy gives Cinderella a wonderful dress.
11. The coach has got six horses.
13. The prince dances with Cinderella.
16. Cinderella loses her shoe.
17. The prince can't see Cinderella.
19. The prince's men go from house to house.
20. Cinderella's stepsisters want to try the shoe on.
21. The shoe fits Cinderella because it is her shoe.
22. The men say to Cinderella, "You are the girl."
24. The prince will marry Cinderella.

5.14 Seite 40

Time (When?)	Place (Where?)	People/Things (Who / What?)	Actions / Events / Facts (What happens?) Reasons (Why?)
at midnight	at the ball	Cinderella prince	dance all night fall in love Cinderella looks beautiful
midnight	at the castle	Cinderella prince	runs away loses one's shoe looks for Cinderella but can't find her
the next morning	at the castle	prince men	go from house to house wants to find Cinderella shoe must fit try on shoe
	at Cinderella's house	men Cinderella sisters	shoe doesn't fit puts on shoe, fits It's Cinderella's shoe
	at the castle	men Cinderella prince	takes Cinderella to the castle marries Cinderella are very happy

5.15 Seite 40

Cinderella lives with her evil stepmother and her two evil stepsisters. She is very unhappy because they hate her and she has to work in the house all day. One day the prince holds a ball at his castle. The two sisters go to the ball. Cinderella can't go. She has got no dress and no shoes. Cinderella starts to cry but suddenly a fairy appears. She gives Cinderella a dress and a pair of shoes. A coach with six horses takes her to the castle. But she must be back home by midnight.
Cinderella dances with the prince and they fall in love. But the prince doesn't know who she is. At 12 o'clock Cinderella runs back home and loses a silk shoe. The prince tells his men to look for the girl all over the town. Finally they find Cinderella because the shoe fits. They marry and live happily ever after.

Lösungen Kapitel 6:

6.1 Seite 41

Lies zuerst den Fragebogen genau durch. Schlage unbekannte Wörter im *dictionary* nach. Kreuze dann die Antworten, die auf dich zutreffen bei *Yes* an. Die anderen erhalten das Kreuz bei *No*. Wenn du alle Fragen beantwortet hast, fertige einen zusammenhängenden Text. Dein Text könnte ungefähr wie folgt lauten:

I live with my parents and I have got one brother. My name is ... and I'm 12 years old. My brother is 14 years old. My parents let me go out with my friends but I have to tell them where I'm going. On Sundays we usually have a big family meal. My father helps with the cooking and my brother and I lay the table and do the washing-up (We don't have a dishwasher). Sometimes my aunt and uncle come to see us and we all play games. On schooldays I have to do my homework after lunch. I usually spend less then two hours on my homework. We have to help at home. We tidy up our bedrooms, go shopping with our father or mother and clean our bikes.

6.2 Seite 43

2. Does he eat bananas? Yes, he does.
3. Does she fly planes? Yes, she does.
4. Does she go to school? Yes, she does.
5. Does he wash the dishes? Yes, he does.

Seite 43 **6.3**

2. Do you speak English?
3. Does Peter ride his bike?
4. Do I know my headmaster?
5. Do you often go to the cinema?
6. Do teachers mark tests?
7. Does the pilot fly planes?
8. Do we play tennis every summer?
9. Do children like sweets?
10. Does she live on the second floor?
11. Does Fred like dogs?

Seite 44 **6.4**

2. Does she go to the bathroom?
3. Does her mother make her breakfast?
4. Do her father and Jimmy come down from the bedroom?
5. Does the dog bark in the garden?
6. Does Jimmy open the door and go into the garden?
7. Do Peter, Brenda and Susan wait at the gate?
8. Do they all go to school?
9. Does it snow in winter?
10. Does Jack remember him?
11. Does he speak English very clearly?
12. Does John laugh a lot?
13. Do we come to class on time?
14. Does your father play football?
15. Do I wash my face every morning?

Seite 45 **6.5**

Hier geht es darum zu sagen, welche Nahrungsmittel du magst und welche nicht. Schlage zuerst die Namen der Nahrungsmittel, die du nicht kennst, in einem *dictionary* nach. Ordne dann die Nahrungsmittel nach Essbarem und Trinkbarem. Schreibe anschließend deine Vorlieben und Abneigungen auf.
Zum Beispiel: I don't like water but I like juice. I like milk but I don't like coffee. I don't like potatoes but I like rice. I like tomatoes but I don't like carrots. I don't like bread but I like cake and chocolate etc.

Seite 46 **6.6**

Mr. Brown likes watching TV but he doesn't like going to work.
Mr. Brown likes cleaning his car but he doesn't like doing the washing-up.
Mr. Brown likes listening to music but he doesn't like reading the newspaper.
Mr. Brown likes going out for walks but he doesn't like driving his car.

Seite 47 **6.7**

Billy: Do you like to go to school?
Brenda: Yes, I do.
Billy: Do you learn English at school?
Brenda: No, I don't.
Brenda: Does your teacher speak German?
Billy: Yes, he does.
Billy: Does your teacher drink milk during the lesson?
Brenda: No, he doesn't.
Brenda: Does your teacher read the newspaper during lesson?
Billy: No, he doesn't.
Billy: Do your parents help you with your homework?
Brenda: Yes, they do.
Billy: Do you and your friends like geography?
Brenda: No, we don't.

Seite 47 **6.8**

Hier sollst du wieder Auskunft über deine Person geben. Beantworte die Fragen bitte jeweils mit *Yes, I do.* oder *No, I don't.* Zum Beispiel:
Do you live with your parents? Yes, I do.
Do you often watch TV? Yes, I do.
Do you like watching football games? No, I don't.
etc.

Lösungen Kapitel 7:

7.1 *Seite 48*

1. head	4. ears	7. thumb / hand
2. nose	5. hair	8. eyes
3. mouth	6. toes / foot	

7.2 *Seite 49*

2. chest / head	6. hair	10. hands
3. legs	7. hand	11. eyes
4. tummy	8. nose	12. fingers
5. head	9. ears	

7.3 *Seite 49*

mouth – call / eat / drink / speak / laugh / smile / kiss / talk
ears – sounds / words / music / teacher
hands – write / carry / lift / point / draw
legs and feet – walk / dance / rush / jump / stand / run / hurry

7.4 *Seite 50*

2. hand	8. toe	14. chest
3. foot	9. nose	15. stomach
4. chin	10. mouth	16. hair
5. knee	11. head	17. thumb
6. ear	12. leg	18. eye
7. finger	13. shoulder	19. forehead

7.5 *Seite 50*

2 – 3 – 1

7.6 *Seite 52*

large nose – große Nase ① ⓒ
He's tall. – Er ist groß. ② Ⓘ
She's wearing glasses. – Sie trägt eine Brille. ③ Ⓡ
small nose – kleine Nase ④ Ⓤ
large eyes – große Augen ⑤ Ⓐ
grey hair – graues Haar ⑥ ⓓ
small mouth – schmaler Mund ⑦ Ⓠ
small eyes – kleine Augen ⑧ Ⓧ
He's tall and fat. – Er ist groß und dick. ⑨ Ⓓ
a square face – ein quadratisches Gesicht ⑩ Ⓖ
ears close to head – eng anliegende Ohren ⑪ Ⓟ
She has a fringe. – Sie hat einen Pony. ⑫ Ⓨ
straight nose – gerade Nase ⑬ Ⓢ
small ears – kleine Ohren ⑭ Ⓦ
He's short. – Er ist klein. ⑮ Ⓥ
She's tall and thin. – Sie ist groß und dünn. ⑯ ⓐ
fair hair – blondes Haar ⑰ Ⓜ
curly hair – lockiges Haar ⑱ Ⓩ
She wears her hair in a ponytail. – Sie trägt einen Pferdeschwanz. ⑲ Ⓔ
He is of medium size. – Er ist mittelgroß. ⑳ Ⓕ
moustache – Schnurrbart ㉑ Ⓒ
His head is bald. – Er ist kahlköpfig. ㉒ Ⓣ
thin lips – dünne Lippen ㉓ Ⓝ
long mouth – breiter Mund ㉔ Ⓚ
round face – rundes Gesicht ㉕ Ⓑ
dark hair – dunkles Haar ㉖ Ⓛ
full lips – volle Lippen ㉗ Ⓙ
He's got a beard. – Er hat einen Bart. ㉘ ⓞ
straight hair – glatte Haare ㉙ Ⓗ
blue eyes – blaue Augen ㉚ ⓑ

Seite 52 **7.7**

von links nach rechts: Jack, Bill, Ned

Seite 53 **7.8**

Bei dieser Übung sollst du auf Englisch eine oder mehrere der abgebildeten Personen beschreiben ohne den Namen zu nennen. Dein Freund soll raten, welche Person(en) du beschreibst.
Beispiel : Coco
I'm thinking of a person. He is a man. He's got a square face with large ears. His mouth is wide, his lips are thin. He's got short, curly hair and a big straight nose. His eyes are big and round. Can you guess which person I'm thinking of?

Edward:
face: round
ears: small, close to head
nose: big
eyes: small
mouth: narrow, moustache
head: bald

Nick:
nose: big
eyes: small
mouth: small
ears: small
hair: curly

Jojo:
face: round
hair: fringe
mouth: wide, big teeth
ears: small
nose: short, small
eyes: small, glasses

Aunt Mary:
face: round
ears: big
eyes: small, glasses
nose: short
mouth: small, narrow
hair: straight

Elizabeth:
face: square
eyes: big, round
nose: small
mouth: wide, full lips
hair: curly, long

Seite 53 **7.9**

Male zuerst ein Bild von dir in den Rahmen oder – wenn vorhanden – klebe ein Foto von dir hinein. Dann fülle die Lücken aus mit Informationen, die dich selbst betreffen.
Beispiel:
This is me. My name is Peter. I think I am just right because I am 110 centimetres tall. My face is round but not too large. My hair is dark and curly. My nose is straight and small and my ears are close to the head. I am quite happy with my looks. My favourite colours are red and yellow. I mostly wear jeans or trousers.

Lösungen Kapitel 8:

Seite 54 **8.1**

Dick is wearing a blue shirt and green trousers.

Seite 55 **8.2**

Fred: shirt, tie, jacket, trousers, socks, shoes
Freda: hat, gloves, pullover, skirt, shoes

Seite 55 **8.3**

3. boots
4. trousers
5. tie
6. socks
7. sandals
8. sweater
9. cardigan
10. blouse
11. shoes
12. jacket

Seite 56 **8.4**

1. trousers
2. boots
3. tracksuit
4. running shoes
5. raincoat
6. sandals
7. umbrella
8. skirt
9. swimming trunks
10. socks
11. shirt
12. gloves
13. cap
14. scarf
15. hat
16. T-shirt
17. waistcoat

8.5 *Seite 57*

half – scarf	fox – socks	dessert – shirt
candles – sandals	tennis racket – jacket	doves – gloves
news – shoes	houses – trousers	goat – coat
cows – blouse	nest – dress	beans – jeans

8.6 *Seite 57*

1. gloves	3. cap / hat	5. scarf / pullover / coat
2. shoes / socks	4. raincoat	6. T-shirt / blouse

8.7 *Seite 58*

2 – 8 – 1 – 6 – 9 – 7 – 10 – 5 – 3 – 4
(von oben links um den Text nach unten rechts)

8.8 *Seite 59*

a patterned dress	a spotted tie	checked trousers
a striped blouse	a long-sleeved cardigan	
a striped skirt	a sleeveless jumper	

8.10 *Seite 60*

a green leather jacket	striped leather shoes	a black skirt
patterned stockings	a pair of sunglasses	a ring in her ear

8.11 *Seite 61*

Richard – boots / jeans / jacket / shirt
Ted – jacket / trousers / shirt / scarf / leather
Peggy – patterned / belt / hat / sandals
Mr. Rich – coat / striped / shirt / plain / gloves
Mrs. Adams – boots / skirt / leather / striped / spotted

8.12 *Seite 62*

boy: a school cap – shirt – a striped tie – jumper – trousers – blazer – shoes
girl: tie – a school blazer – blouse – skirt – socks – shoes

8.13 *Seite 62*

Einige Schulen in Deutschland schreiben inzwischen eine bestimmte Schulkleidung vor. Wenn das auf dich zutrifft, beschreibe deine Schulkleidung. Wenn nicht – beschreibe, was du trägst, wenn du zur Schule gehst.

Lösungen Kapitel 9:

9.1 *Seite 63*

detached house / flat / cottage / farmhouse / castle / ghost / Eskimo / igloo / dog / kennel

9.2 *Seite 64*

Trage zuerst die Angaben, die auf dich zutreffen, in die Lücken ein. Benutze dann deine Angaben und beschreibe dein Heim.
Zum Beispiel: Today I want to tell you about the block of flats where I live. My home is not far from my school. It is on the second floor. There are six rooms. Our house has got a large garden at the back where children can play. Our flat has got a balcony, too. Sometimes my mother uses it for hanging out the washing. In the summertime we often have our meals on the balcony.

9.4 *Seite 65*

1. door	4. grass	7. roof
2. chimney	5. walls	8. a window
3. gate	6. garage	9. tree

Seite 66 **9.5**

1. He lives in a semi-detached house.
2. There are seven rooms altogether.
3. He is happy because he can watch people from his window and he can play in the loft and in the garden.
4. The first room is the hall.
5. They eat their meals in the living room on Sundays and Peter watches television there and listens to his parents' stereo.
6. They have their meals in the kitchen on weekdays.
7. He can see people passing their house.
8. Yes, there is. It's the loft.
9. The washing machine is in the cellar.
10. Yes, there is a small back garden.

Seite 68 **9.6**

Michael's description is right.

Seite 69 **9.7**

2. We have breakfast in the kitchen.
3. I watch television in the living room.
4. She writes a letter in the living room.
5. We eat a sandwich in the kitchen.
6. She has a shower in the bathroom.
7. They brush their teeth in the bathroom.
8. We play table tennis in the garden.
9. They put on their clothes in the bedroom.
10. He reads a book in the living room.

Seite 70 **9.8**

2. The kitchen is downstairs on the ground floor.
3. The parent's bedroom is upstairs on the second floor.
4. The hall is downstairs on the ground floor.
5. The toilet is upstairs on the first floor.
6. Mary's room is upstairs in the loft.

Seite 70 **9.9**

Kreuze zuerst an, in welchem Raum du und deine Familie welche Aktivitäten tätigt. Schreibe dann einen Text über das, was du und deine Familie in welchen Räumen tut.
Zum Beispiel:
I sleep in my room. There are lots of toys in my room. I have pictures and posters on the walls. We usually eat in the living room but we have breakfast in the kitchen. We often sit in the garden when the weather is fine. My favourite place is the living room because I listen to CDs and we watch TV there.

Seite 71 **9.10**

The room belongs to Carol.

Bevor du dich entscheidest, wem der Raum gehört, sieh dir das Bild genau an und schreibe auf, welche Aktivitäten das Mädchen aus dem Zimmer tut.
She plays tennis. She wears jeans. She rides a bicycle. She watches TV. She collects teapots. She speaks French and German. She plays the guitar. She drinks Coke and tea. She likes chocolate, apples, peanuts and tomato soup.

Seite 72 **9.11**

Wenn du herausfinden möchtest, ob du lieber in der Stadt oder auf dem Land wohnst, beantworte zunächst die Fragen und notiere dir die Punkte. Zähle dann die Punkte zusammen und lies, was für ein Typ du bist.

Lösungen Kapitel 14:

14.2 *Seite 100*

[iː]: sheep, bees, seat, knee, leaf, tree
[ɪə]: year, beer, near, tear, hear
[eə]: bear, hair, pair, where, air, there
[ɜː]: bum, world, bird, work, learn, third

14.4 *Seite 103*

[eɪ] = baby, eight, snake, rain, way, play
[æ] = camp, man, cap, hat, gas, sad
[e] = pet, ten, desk
[əʊ] = ghost, bowl
[ɜː] = girl
[ɪ] = pin, milk, mill, pig
[aɪ] = sign, knife, like, pie, sky, time
[uː] = shoe, who, pool, two
[iː] = knee, bee
[ɒ] = hot, fox, stocking, stop
[ʊ] = foot, book

Register

f. bedeutet: Du findest das Stichwort auf dieser und auf der folgenden Seite.

ff. bedeutet: Du findest das Stichwort auf dieser und auf mehreren folgenden Seiten.

H

J

K

L

M

N

O

P

Q

R

S

T

V

W

Z